Action Research
in Education

Mary McAteer

SAGE

Los Angeles | London | New Delhi
Singapore | Washington DC

Los Angeles | London | New Delhi
Singapore | Washington DC

SAGE Publications Ltd
1 Oliver's Yard
55 City Road
London EC1Y 1SP

SAGE Publications Inc.
2455 Teller Road
Thousand Oaks, California 91320

SAGE Publications India Pvt Ltd
B 1/I 1 Mohan Cooperative Industrial Area
Mathura Road
New Delhi 110 044

SAGE Publications Asia-Pacific Pte Ltd
3 Church Street
#10-04 Samsung Hub
Singapore 049483

Editor: Marianne Lagrange
Assistant editor: Kathryn Bromwich
Production editor: Jeanette Graham
Copyeditor: Carol Lucas
Proofreader: Isabel Kirkwood
Indexer: Anne Solomito
Marketing manager: Catherine Slinn
Cover design: Wendy Scott
Typeset by: C&M Digitals (P) Ltd, Chennai, India
Printed in Great Britain by MPG Printgroup, UK

Library of Congress Control Number: 2012930228

British Library Cataloguing in Publication data

A catalogue record for this book is available from
the British Library

MIX
Paper from
responsible sources
FSC
www.fsc.org   FSC® C018575

ISBN 978-1-4462-4105-9
ISBN 978-1-4462-4106-6 (pbk)

Acti... ...ch
in Ed

Research Methods in Education

Each book in this series maps the territory of a key research approach or topic in order to help readers progress from beginner to advanced researcher:

Each book aims to provide a definitive, market-leading overview and to present a blend of theory and practice with a critical edge. All titles in the series are written for Masters-level students anywhere and are intended to be useful to the many diverse constituencies interested in research on education and related areas.

Titles in the series:

Atkins & Wallace	*Qualitative Research in Education*
Hamilton & Corbett-Whittier	*Using Case Study in Education Research*
McAteer	*Action Research in Education*
Mills & Morton	*Ethnography in Education*

Access the additional resources here:
http://www.sagepub.co.uk/beraseries.sp

BRITISH EDUCATIONAL RESEARCH ASSOCIATION

Los Angeles | London | New Delhi
Singapore | Washington DC

CONTENTS

ABOUT THE AUTHOR

Mary McAteer has worked for over 30 years as a teacher, local authority consultant and educator, in a range of senior pastoral and curriculum roles. Since 1999 she has held posts as Senior Lecturer and Principal Lecturer, and programme lead for Master's Level Professional Development Programmes in two different universities. Her current post is Director of the Mathematics Specialist Teacher (MaST) programme in Edge Hill University, where she also has responsibility for teaching Research Methods and supervising doctoral students. Her passion for action research stems from her own postgraduate study both at Master's and Doctoral level, and has developed through supporting students through a range of action research studies.

Recent publications include 'Theory generative approaches in practitioner research', in J. Adams, M. Cochrane and L. Dunne (eds) (2011) *Applying Theory to Educational Research: An Introductory Approach with Case Studies,* Oxford: Wiley Blackwell, and McAteer, M. (ed) (2012) *Improving Primary Mathematics Teaching and Learning.* Berkshire: Open University Press.

ACKNOWLEDGEMENTS

Grateful thanks are due to Kathryn Bromwich and all the team at Sage who have so patiently supported me through the writing of this book. Likewise, I wish to thank all at BERA involved in the commissioning of it and in providing initial feedback on the proposal. To all those reviewers who have provided feedback on early drafts, I wish also to express my grateful thanks.

Throughout this book I have drawn on my experiences as an action research student, practitioner and tutor/supervisor. I have had the great fortune and privilege to work with a wide variety of colleagues in a number of universities, and an even wider range of students, on action research and other professional development programmes. Conversations, discussions and collaborations with all of them have been significant in enriching and shaping my own knowledge, beliefs and values.

I was first introduced to the British Educational Research Association (BERA) and the Collaborative Action Research Network (CARN) while a student at the University of Ulster. My grateful thanks are extended to my DPhil supervisor, Dr Barry Hutchinson, for supporting my thinking and putting me in touch with two such wonderful support networks. CARN, as a network dedicated to action research, has played a particularly big role for me, and one member in particular, Kath Green was both a supportive and challenging dear friend. Her passion for conversation and life stories, her sense of respect for all, her particular support for new conference presenters were a key part of the annual CARN conference. Described by colleagues as someone who 'embodied the heart of CARN' and who 'treated life as an opportunity for learning', she believed passionately that the simple act of raising questions can raise the level of discourse. Her life (1946–2007) represented a synthesis of intellect and emotion, and has left a quiet, gentle but powerful legacy to those who knew her. Chapter 5 is written in her memory and with grateful thanks for her influence. It is written in the hope that she would have approved, and in the knowledge that, had she not, then it would have provided fodder for a rich and enriching conversation and learning experience.

The case studies in this book are derived from the following unpublished MSc Dissertations, University of Ulster:

McCay, M.B. (2003) *Addressing Underachievement: Giving students a voice.*
McGlinchey, M. (2002) *Teachers for education, Education for teachers: Promoting a spirit of curiosity, inquiry and reflection in science, that touches teachers and pupils alike.*
Wilson, R. (2003) *How can I improve the quality of talk in my role play corner?*
Vaughan, C. (2003) *Parents as partners in the educational experiences of young children.*

INTRODUCTION AND OVERVIEW

This book provides both theoretical perspectives and practical examples for practitioners of action research in education-based contexts. A key feature of the book is the articulation of the close linkage between theory and practice, the theory-generative nature of action research and the illustration of theoretical perspectives and dilemmas through the use of examples drawn from practice. In the current climate of accountability, competing agendas can cause dilemmas and tensions for practitioners engaging in action research. Bringing together perspectives from action research tutors and practitioners whose lives have been changed by action research studies, the book provides a rigorous practical and theoretical guide, while also exploring the tensions and dilemmas in this type of research. Drawing on Elliott's (1991) concept of the essentially change-inducing nature of action research, cases studies illustrate and explore the potential for change in real educational situations.

Who is this book for?

If you are interested in action research as a means to professional learning and the improvement of professional practice in education, then regardless of your job role, this book is for you. It is primarily aimed at those undertaking postgraduate study (which could be during initial teacher training or professional development programmes), in that it explores the scholarship of action research, and discusses the development of the more formal academic skills that might be required in undertaking such a programme. However, each chapter is also well illustrated with case study examples, giving a clear insight into the actual practice of action research, and if your action research project is not part of a postgraduate study programme, you will still find much of use in the book. Course tutors and project leaders will be able to draw on both the theoretical and practical materials in the book as they support students and mentees through projects.

Structure of the book

Section 1 of the book (Getting to Know Action Research) comprises two chapters, written to address some of the more theoretical discussions and debates around contemporary action research in education. The book opens with a chapter locating action research in both its historical and epistemological roots, while identifying its contemporary use, and some of the tensions inherent in that. The main function of this chapter is to identify just what action research is and, importantly, is not. It seeks to address the current use and misuse of the term by exploring both the academic integrity of action research as a valid research methodology, and the current focus on teacher (and other practitioner) research initiatives in schools and settings which often have as their main purpose the evaluation of education policy and initiatives.

The second chapter provides a synoptic overview of a range of models of and perspectives on action research, introducing some of its philosophical underpinnings. Drawing also on the nature and role of reflection in action research, the chapter will resonate with and be relevant to teachers and educators at all stages in their careers. The complexity and messiness of action research as an organic human social activity are explored, leading to a discussion of the ethical and moral dimensions of action research as a value-laden process.

Section 2 (Doing Action Research) comprises Chapters 3 to 7; each taking a particular aspect of the action research process, teasing out both the practical and theoretical issues involved (and the relationship between them) through case studies from practice. Each chapter comprises an introductory overview, case studies with a narrative and theoretical commentary, prompts for personal reflection and a concluding summary section. In each of these chapters, case studies have been drawn from real contexts. In some cases the narrative is what Bold (2012) would call a constructed narrative, in that it may draw two or three examples together into a single case in order to more fully illustrate the point being made, and also to protect identity.

Section 3 (Sharing Action Research) contains the final chapter, which is devoted to the ways in which action research reports and the action research process may be shared and disseminated. Illustrations of the important professional learning that can occur in projects serve to provide a backdrop against which to suggest ways in which this powerful professional learning can be shared. Case studies used in this chapter come from published masters dissertations, and have been completed by teachers working in a range of contexts. The chapter concludes by reminding action researchers that even a 'final report', like action research itself, is still a work in progress.

Note on style

It should be noted that throughout the book, extracts from authentic research journals are presented as they have been written, as examples of personal reflective notes, and may at times be relatively informal in style. It is not unusual for action research reports to include such extracts in their original form, as their informality can convey something of their tone which the 'tidied' text would not.

Additional online resources can be found at:
www.sagepub.co.uk/beraseries.sp

SECTION 1

GETTING TO KNOW ACTION RESEARCH

CHAPTER 1

WHAT IS THIS THING CALLED ACTION RESEARCH?

The changing context of educational practice

Reflecting on and learning from our practice is perhaps the most natural and innate process in the business of being human. For a young child it is a completely instinctive process, so that the subtle changes in position which promote improved balance become innately understood and developed in any toddler in the early days of learning to walk or get around. Likewise, the processes of communication become honed and polished as we listen to our own voice and those of others, reviewing and refining our own in order to improve our communication practice. Gaining mobility and communication skills are highly situated, contextualised activities, and develop in different ways according to that contextualised need. If we take 'learning to talk' as an example, we can see that even within a relatively small geographical area, variations of syntax, accent, sophistication and extent of vocabulary and so forth are clearly evident. These variations will arise, in general, as a result of the beginning talker trying to find the best way of communicating within their own particular context.

The fact is, a small child learns a great deal about how to make its own way into the world without being formally taught, instinctively reflects on practice trying to make it better, and has a fairly egocentric world-view. It really is 'all about me' for a young child. It could be said perhaps that the developing infant instinctively understands the nature and potency of action research.

For many teachers or other education practitioners, however, action research, presented to them through the academic processes of their initial and continuing education, can prove quite a philosophical challenge. Somewhere between infancy and adulthood, we subvert (and occasionally lose) our naive understandings of the world, and become entangled in the processes and procedures of a more formal learning environment. As schooling becomes more ritualised and routinised, we begin to look to those rituals and routines as *sources* of learning, rather than *organisational strategies* for it. The tendency to ask how to do something, rather than explore the nature of that something, is, in a way, a pragmatic response to the reality and busy-ness of life. The corollary of this, though, is that it can be an inhibitory response in terms of learning. Without such a questioning approach, our engagement with concepts and processes can remain at a relatively superficial level.

Recent changes in education

Reflecting on the past 30 years in terms of school management, government policies and initiatives, we can see that there has been a significant change in ways in which schools are managed. The introduction of a national curriculum following the 1988 Education Reform Act, paved the way for a raft of associated policies and procedures, from guides to pedagogy, assessment and record-keeping, to classroom management, differentiation and, indeed, school management. The transition to this more heavily prescribed and bureaucratised approach to education was challenging for many teachers in its early stages, and in particular for those who had worked for a significant number of years under a much more flexible regime. For many, it represented a loss of autonomy and the erosion of both the place and the value of their 'professional judgement'. In the words of Hutchinson and Whitehouse, the education reforms did 'not brook any questioning' (1999: 153).

While subsequent reviews have made changes in the content and scope of curriculum legislation, the increase in bureaucracy continues to impact strongly on our concept of what contemporary schooling looks like and how it is organised. Alongside this growth in bureaucracy there was also the development of a new language. Learning styles, the three-part lesson, curriculum delivery, assessment for learning, best practice, scaffolding and a raft of other new terms became part of the educational vocabulary. Words like 'value added', 'accountability', 'buy in' and 'stakeholders' were further additions and, for many teachers, suggestive of a change in both the focus and the values of contemporary education. Once only associated with marketisation and commercial venture, they became subsumed into the language of educational processes, bringing with them a feeling that education was being commodified in a way that was hitherto unknown for many teachers, and heralded significant philosophical challenges. The very art of teaching seemed to be under attack. In secondary schools, there were concerns about how teachers would cope with pupils suddenly facing the demands of a 'balanced curriculum', where they were forced to do subjects from within each of five curricular areas until the age of 16. In primary schools, the introduction of compulsory science and technology was perhaps the biggest area of anxiety for teachers.

The highly prescriptive programmes of study with their complex levels and statements of attainment suggested to teachers that the main function of teaching now was to ensure that all children reached these levels, and that the appropriate boxes were ticked in order to demonstrate that. Effective teachers would deliver the appropriate content to pupils (described by one of my colleagues at the time as the 'deliverology' model of education) and prepare them for assessment tasks which had become more standardised, thus enabling the establishment of school league tables so that schools could be compared, like for like, against each other. These tables allowed parents also to choose schools for their children, making judgements on the basis of the school's measured performance. The 'free market' model of education had clearly arrived.

Changing schools, changing teachers

Alongside curricular and organisational changes there was also a growing expectation that teachers would engage in continuing professional development throughout their career. From the early 1980s, part-time, in-service Bachelor of Education (BEd) programmes, which enabled all teachers to hold graduate-level qualifications, became increasingly popular as the proportion of graduate-qualified teachers joined the profession, and non-graduates felt the need to upgrade their qualifications, and thereby their job and promotion prospects. (Prior to that time, teacher training enabled holders of the earlier Certificate of Education to teach in primary and secondary schools.) It was not long before there was a demand for master's level professional development programmes, and most university faculties of education developed diploma and master's programmes to meet this demand. While this provision was very much driven by individual teacher needs and desires, it did much to embed the notion of postgraduate professional development into the culture of schools and settings. The mid-1990s saw a change in the funding arrangements for such provision, and a subsequent move towards partnership arrangements between universities and other providers to ensure that the provision matched need on a more organisational than individual level. The notion of school-driven professional development through postgraduate programmes was consolidated by then, and subsequent funding arrangements were, in the main, centred on postgraduate, award-bearing provision.

Initiatives in England, such as the introduction of funded Postgraduate Professional Development (PPD) opportunities by the (then) Training and Development Agency (TDA) from 2006 to 2011, the Master's in Teaching and Learning introduced in 2008 and the newly introduced National Scholarship Scheme for Professional Development, all suggested that award-bearing, master's-level provision was a valued and valuable option. The Chartered Teacher Pathway in Scotland, and the current development in Wales of a Master's in Educational Practice similarly attest to the desirability and the potency of highly contextualised professional development. Their designation as master's-level courses, rather than traditional in-service training (INSET) programmes which tended to train teachers in the use of specific resources or approaches (normally being completed in one-day or half-day sessions) suggest that academic rigour is a valuable feature.

While there have been recent changes in legislation and funding in England (the PPD funding stream has now been discontinued), there is still a focus on high-quality professional development for practising teachers (often linked to a specific subject or pedagogic focus). The introduction of the National Scholarship Scheme in 2011, which called for applicants who wanted to 'use this money for Master's level development, or other highly valuable opportunities, such as subject specific seminars', was as a direct result of the 2010 Schools White Paper, '*The Importance of Teaching*'. Master's-level professional development continues to be a central strand in educational initiatives and policy-making.

Rooting these programmes and initiatives in practitioner research means that, at present, most schools in the UK will have some form of small-scale practitioner research project in place. Similar experiences are to be found in a range of countries, from Australia to North America, with journals such as *Educational Action Research*, *Action Research*, *Reflective Practice* regularly featuring articles which have arisen from these projects. A range of networks exists to provide support for action researchers, and conferences such as the annual Collaborative Action Research Network (CARN) actively encourage presentation from such work. While it is clear that all such projects have the potential to support practitioners and their schools, and are often branded as 'action research' in an all-encompassing way, it is important that we clarify what is and, probably more importantly, what is not action research.

The relationship between practitioner research and action research

For most teachers and other educational practitioners, Initial Teacher Education (ITE) and continuing professional development (CPD) work offer opportunities to engage in practitioner research. In addition to research experiences embedded in programmes of (academic) study, they also form part of other professional development, in-service courses. The National College offers opportunities for English teachers, aspiring and in-post school leaders to undertake recognised development programmes, many of which incorporate practitioner research elements. Similarly, the International Leadership and Management Program offers practitioner-research based programmes for school and college leaders in international schools.

The term 'action research' is often used in relation to the projects teachers undertake as part of these professional development programmes, regardless of whether their work is of an action research nature or not. At one level, this broad-brush understanding of action research can be seen as a pragmatic approach which serves the purpose of engaging people in activities that do explore and seek to understand practice and its impact. At another level, however, the potential for such project work to be inaccurately described and lacking in the intellectual rigour of a specific framework does no service to the programmes themselves, the participants nor, indeed, to the public face of action research and other practitioner research approaches. In a climate where deeply encultured approaches to understanding 'research' as a scientific process underpinned by numbers and percentages have led to a view of more narrative and naturalistic approaches to research as being 'not real research' and descriptions of such research approaches in a language which is at best, loose and, at worst, inaccurate, their public acceptance is made more problematic and their validity suspect. For this reason, this chapter seeks to articulate the provenance and nature of action research, and to clarify its formulation as a specific, rigorous and methodologically appropriate form of practice-based research. All practitioner research requires its participants to 'to engage with both "theoretical" and "practical" knowledge moving seamlessly between the two' (Groundwater-Smith and Mockler, 2006: 107), but action research makes a further demand. It requires not only the critical reflection on practice and theory–practice conversation, but also it designates ongoing and evolving action as part of that process. We will develop this later in the chapter, and throughout the book, but first a brief look at the nature of 'research' itself, and where practitioner research and action research fit into this.

The research continuum

It is perhaps helpful to start by taking a brief look at the nature of research and its manifestations. 'Research' may be thought of as a con- tinuum of approaches, with scientific, or positivistic, research at one end, and the more naturalistic and interpretive approaches at the other. An example of scientific research is that which is carried out in medical drug trials, where the notion of 'objectivity' is embedded in the philosophy, and where the design of the project will normally involve some form of blind testing and/or control group, with the findings used to generate a generalisable 'truth'. Thus, trials suggest that 98 per cent of all patients will achieve a significant reduction of symptoms when taking drug X. Likewise, figures suggesting that only 1 per cent of those taking the drug are likely to suffer any unpleasant side effects, and of these side effects, none has been found to be medically worrying, can be used to assure us of its safety. Results such as this can inform the decision of a company to launch the drug, and brand it as safe. Similarly, engineering science may seek to produce a set of experimental results which can then be generalised. Repeated tests on particular materials allow engineers to choose specific materials and dimensions for specialist uses, knowing that they have proof of their efficacy in such uses. Proof is a word that is often found in scientific experimentation and research. I am not saying here of course that purely exploratory scientific research does not take place. What I am saying is that much experimental science and research is of the type that discovers 'truths' and seeks to 'prove'. It can be described, therefore, as belonging to the positivistic research paradigm. In other words, its underpinning philosophy is that knowledge is derived from the interrogation and verification of empirical data.

At the other end of this continuum of research approaches we find the more naturalistic and interpretive approaches. This end of the continuum is sometimes described as 'anti-positivistic' (although I often feel that is a confrontational term, and prefer 'non-positivistic') and is generally under- stood as the set of research approaches which includes phenomenological, ethnomethodological and biographical approaches. Practitioner research is located at this end of the continuum. The term is broad in scope, and covers a range of approaches which tend to be characterised by a desire to explore, explain or describe practice. Data collected tends to be more qualitative than quantitative in nature, and the resultant report will often seek to identify key features of the practice, particular insights into practice, or recommendations for future practice. The practitioner case study is a good example of this type of research. Habermas, writing in 1970, suggests a tripartite typology of knowledge: empirical and analytical; hermeneutic (interpretive or explanatory) and historical; and critical knowledge. Practitioner research is usually thought of as residing in the hermeneutic and historical category. In newly identifying 'critical knowledge' as a valid category, Habermas paved the way for those researchers and theorists who felt that other paradigms did not fully address the need to either critique ideology, nor effectively deal with the practice-based knowledge incorporated in the day to day lives of people. This brings us to an introduction to the very specific nature of action research.

The location of action research on the continuum

While action research is usually considered to reside under the broad umbrella of 'practitioner research', its proponents would suggest that while it does indeed share some features of practitioner research, and does produce historical and hermeunetic knowledge, it does more than this. Its inextricable practice–theory relationship, and its acknowledged location of the researcher and the context right at the centre of both the research and the practice, suggest that it more properly resides within the critical knowledge category. It both explores and theorises practice, changes, evaluates and develops practice, provides a platform from which to critique ideology, and in doing so incorporates a moral as well as an epistemological dimension to the research. In its most simple form, it has its roots in the question 'How can I improve my practice', and in this way it implies a range of sub-questions from 'Why should I improve?' to 'what does improvement mean?' and 'Where does my practice and possible changes reside in a policy, theoretical and ideological framework?'. The action and the research, the theory and the practice become unified in questions of 'ought' rather than 'can'. The discussion and debate around such matters is important, but can be challenging, particularly for the action researcher. Getting caught up in the deeper philosophical conversation may indeed inhibit the potential for the novice researcher to 'get going' on their project. The challenge at this stage, therefore, is to develop sufficient understanding on a philosophical basis, but at the same time leave the reader feeling enabled and empowered to actually undertake the research with integrity. As is the case in real action research projects, philosophical issues will arise along the way, so rather than abstract them from their environment, we will discuss and explore them in the context of the case studies in subsequent chapters.

For this reason, I wish to move the focus back now to the more pragmatic matters of action research. Framing this discussion in Elliott's (1991: 49) notion that 'the fundamental aim of action research is to improve practice' is perhaps a good starting point in that it immediately makes a clear and explicit link to practice and, perhaps more so than any other statement of paradigmatic purpose, speaks loud and clear to the practitioner, be that a teacher in training, a teacher or teaching assistant in the classroom, a school leader or any other practitioner. Educational provision takes place in an increasingly broad range of settings and contexts, and while the words 'school' and 'teacher' are frequently used throughout the book, they should be understood as inclusive of all settings and practitioners. I am also conscious that, particularly for younger readers, some of the references in this chapter (and Chapter 2) may seem dated. I have deliberately chosen, however, to refer to the key works of some of the most important protagonists of action research in its current usage in schools and other educational settings. While the term 'active research' is familiar to perhaps all educational practitioners at present, in the 1970s and 1980s, it was just beginning to emerge as the approach of choice for teachers in schools, for health and social work professionals, and others, such as community and youth workers. Most of the current usage of action research draws heavily on texts written at this time, many of which speak directly to the needs and concerns of teachers in a relevant and accessible way, assuming no prior knowledge of the approach. They are still highly valuable texts and, from my perspective, a highly effective way to learn not only how to 'do' action research, but also how to 'think' action research.

The development of action research

Locating action research both historically and philosophically is important in helping us understand not only where action research has come from, but also how it has evolved to meet the specific needs and concerns of practitioners.

Initially thought to have been developed for the purposes of educational improvement by Corey (1953) from the work of Lewin in the 1940s, the modern usage of action research owes much to the work of Stenhouse, in the 1970s, who suggested that the work of the teacher be researched, and by teachers themselves. He felt, however, that this study or research should be supported and guided by the use of professional researchers who would also choose the focus for the research (Stenhouse, 1975).

The model of practitioner research which located the research issue with the teacher's own initial concern was developed by Elliott in the late 1970s, suggesting that either the teacher could carry out the research or could commission someone else to do it. In either case, the research was an effort to understand 'the social situation in which the participant finds himself' (Elliott, 1978: 355), and was thus located in the teacher's intrinsic, rather than the researcher's external, concerns. This model was further developed in later work by Elliott and others, and unlike the traditional positivistic or scientific model of research, focused on the reciprocal relationship between theory and practice. This relationship was expounded in his 1981 paper advising that 'theories are not validated independently and then applied to practice. They are validated through practice.' (Elliott, 1981: 1)

In order to maintain the reciprocation between research and action, between theory and practice, action research, again unlike positivistic research (and, indeed, unlike most other forms of practitioner research) is operationally cyclical, the findings of each cycle informing the planning and carrying out of the next. While Chapter 2 deals with some of the representations of the action research cycle, it is important to note that most are based on the models illustrated by Kemmis and McTaggart (1981) or Elliott (1981, 1991). Their demonstration of the cyclical and reciprocal interaction between research and findings, between action and theory, is perhaps best summed up by Winter who suggests that while 'the possibility of change is grounded in the distinction between action and research, it requires equally an intimate and principled linkage between the two, in order that the "findings" of research can be translatable back into the world of action' (Winter, 1987: 21). Thus, the action researcher is both practical and theoretical in approach. Each aspect of the research depends on and supports the development of the other, providing an almost conversational relationship between them. This rather elegant articulation of what Winter (1987) describes as the essential reciprocity between research and action, between theory and practice, raises important issues about the epistemological and axiological or value-based nature of action research. Its immediate question however, is to the nature and place of theory in research.

Theory in action research

In many if not most approaches to research, even in the field of social sciences, research is something done *on* practice or *applied to* practice.

There will normally be some degree of distance and detachment between the researcher and the 'subject' of that research (who may be a practitioner in the field), hence allowing a claim to objectivity. There will almost certainly be epistemological distance between the researcher and the practitioner during the research period, and it is likely that the carrying out of their roles and functions depends on differing epistemological stances. These differing roles and stances also suggest distance between the resulting theories and associated changed practices. By this I mean that theories are traditionally devised by a researcher who is part of a research community rather than part of the practitioner community being researched. This research methodology (and 'methodology' is more than just 'method', as we explore in Chapter 2) is likely to have a different epistemology to the practice it researches, and may therefore be distanced in its beliefs and values as well as its intellectual standpoint.

A further feature about this type of research is that it is usually carried out by outside academics or trained researchers and, as such, assumes, or is given, prescriptive authority over existing practice. Such a situation can have the effect of either antagonising or producing unquestioning conformity in practitioners. These are familiar responses in many school communities where teachers feel that their professional knowledge and judgement are undervalued, and their theoretical knowledge insufficient. Additionally, for many teachers and other practitioners, the resulting theory from research of this nature is not quite the match for their own context and specific practice that it might be. It is not uncommon for school improvement officers, on presenting a research-based solution to 'the problem of underachievement/demotivation/ behaviour, etc.', to be faced with 'that would be all very well if my school/class . . .'. In dealing with real-world, small-scale concerns, context is everything.

Thus, most research presents an implied hierarchy, suggestive of the dominance of theory over practice. For teachers and other practitioners, this can seem somewhat denigratory of that which they value profoundly. Their own practical knowledge (a form of what Elliott and others would call 'practical philosophy'), shaped and honed by the experience of the practice, and associated thoughtfulness about that practice, is held in high esteem in both their own perception and within their profession.

Action research, in understanding theory as an essential part of practice, and indeed derived from it, seeks to redress this balance and speak to both the needs and the values of practitioners. Drawing heavily on the concept of 'reflective practice', it is also epistemologically aligned to the practice of teachers. Indeed, in attempting to dissolve the distinctions between theory and practice, and with an acknowledged practice-improvement stance, it

can (and, some would argue, should) result in the clarification of the practitioner's own beliefs, values and intellectual standpoint.

Further, in becoming a means through which practitioners can theorise their practice in collaboration with peers, pupils and others, it
becomes both a democratic and democratising process, and raises
important questions about the nature of knowledge, particularly that
which is practice based.

Democracy in action research and the nature of knowledge

A move away from the theory-dominant hierarchy of many other approaches
to research to a more democratic process, changes the relationship between
theory and practice, and offers opportunities through which to question
knowledge of practice, what it means, how it is constructed/derived and
what use it is. The almost conversational relationship between theory and
practice indicated in action research is suggestive of greater provisionality
in our understanding of what counts as knowledge, than more positivistic
approaches would imply. We have a deep cultural understanding of the
nature of knowledge as 'scientific', based on truths and proofs, characterised, and indeed validated by, concepts of subjectivity, and action research
as a way of knowing, presents us with challenges in this respect. Interestingly though, our cultural notion of science and scientific, and our
understanding of their definitiveness, are probably based more on perception than actuality. Philosophers and practitioners of science recognise not
only the provisionality of scientific knowledge, but that it is necessary for
scientists to understand the need for challenge in their work. Popper,
writing in the late 1950s, comments that science 'is not a knowledge
(episteme): it can never claim to have attained truth, or even a substitute
for it' (Popper, 1959: 278). Indeed, searching for a single truth suggests a
search for confirmatory evidence (only), and leads to what Popper calls
a 'wrong view of science' which 'betrays itself in the craving to be right'
(Popper, 1968: 281). Likewise, Kuhn suggests that the interpretations by
scientists are always provisional and, indeed, often controversial in nature,
and advocates the need for science to 'prepare the way for its own change'
(Kuhn, 1970: 65).

This concept of preparing the way for its own change is one which is
central to the notion and practice of action research. Returning to Elliott's
(1991) definition of action research as a means to improve practice, we can
begin to move from a problem-solving, responsive strategy, to one which
is problem-posing, or problematising, continually subjecting practice to

critical inquiry, challenging the 'taken for granted' and consciously seeking alternative perspectives as a means through which to generate the
understanding that will bring practical improvements into being.

Problem posing and generating theory

While much research in education is conducted along para-scientific lines
in that it uses concepts and values such as proof, replicability, sampling,
objectivity and so forth, action research draws upon other strategies and
concepts, such as authenticity and truth, individual voice, relatability and
so on. These concepts are all discussed in later chapters. Significantly, the
centrality of 'I' in action research is key to its nature and its potency. Its
situation is right at the heart of practitioners' own practice, and it subjects
itself to continued testing and validation through that process. In essence,
the research itself becomes part of the practice researched, while the
practice becomes a research practice. The relationship is such that reflection is the critical process that allows both action and research their
authenticity in retheorising action or practice as research, and research as
practice or action. Winter puts it elegantly, saying:

> [T]he theoretical necessity of a reflexive conception of research's relation
> to action, so that their relationship may be theorised in ways which pre-
> serves the authenticity of both, i.e. which preserves research's capacity for
> achieving a critical distance from action, AND preserves action's intelligi-
> bility, as a creative, rather than a causally determined response to interpre-
> tive meaning. (Winter, 1987: 22)

Action research therefore transforms both the nature and the possibilities
of both action and research.

Reflection and action research

It would be remiss to discuss action research, even in a perfunctory manner, without discussing reflective practice. Described by Day (1993: 83) as
a 'necessary but not sufficient condition for professional development' he
views reflection without some imperative to action, as a process unlikely
to lead to change. Recognising the need to become immersed in the
(crucially important) messiness and complexity of practice (the 'swampy
lowlands'), he also cites Schön (1983) in differentiating between those
who do make this choice, and those for whom the choice is 'solid technical competence', concluding that 'It is tempting to suggest that the
future for those who wish to contribute to professional development lies in

choosing the lowlands' (Day, 1993: 94). Similarly, while reflection is a necessary starting point for action research, without taking it forward through the full action research cycle the potential for change and improvement is lost. Chapter 2 explores in more detail the nature of reflection in an action research practice and ways in which its quality can be enhanced.

This chapter has provided a very brief overview of some of the conceptual and philosophical underpinnings of action research. It locates this form of practitioner research firmly in both an epistemological and a practice perspective, thus demonstrating its academic provenance and its relevance to practice. Chapter 2 develops these concepts further as you are introduced to models of 'doing' action research.

I have deliberately chosen not to deal with the issue of alternative notions of action research. As you engage in further reading during your studies, you will become aware of some alternative perspectives, in particular, the debate as to whether or not 'educational', 'educative' and 'social science' are interchangeable descriptors of action research. You will also come across 'emancipatory', 'participatory' and 'first and second order' action research, and various other descriptors. There are interesting debates to be had around these, and at one level they are important in your development as someone who 'thinks' action research, but they are also time-consuming, particularly if you are engaged in small-scale studies in education. Zeichner's cautionary note to teachers is apposite here:

> [A] lot of this discourse, although highly informative in an academic sense, is essentially irrelevant to many of those who actually engage in action research . . .
>
> There are many different cultures of action research and it seems to me that an awful lot of time and energy is wasted in arguing over who are the 'real' action researchers and who are the imposters . . . (Zeichner, 1993: 200–1)

The next chapter explores some of the pragmatics of undertaking action research, discussing models and approaches, and raises the most fundamental of all questions in relation to action research: 'How do I know that action research is the correct methodology for me?'

Further reading

McNiff, J. and Whitehead, J. (2011) *All You Need to Know about Action Research*. London: Sage.

Like all of the many books by McNiff and Whitehead, this book is highly accessible to a range of readers. Novice action researchers will find its structure easy to follow and its personal voice supportive of their own first-person writing. The book is divided into seven sections, each framed with a first-person question such as 'How do I test and critique my knowledge?'

Pine, G. (2009) *Teacher Action Research: Building Knowledge Democracies*. London: Sage.

This is in many ways a 'harder read' than the McNiff and Whitehead text mentioned above. That said, its easy combination of practical and theoretical matters enhances its accessibility. The book will be of particular use to those readers who, having gained an initial insight into action research, wish to further develop their theoretical understanding.

Combining a sound philosophical and epistemological analysis of the conceptual bases of action research, this text also addresses pragmatic and practical matters in a way that is accessible to practitioner researchers. Beginning action researchers will find it both supportive, but with appropriate intellectual challenge. The structure of the book, in making 'Practicing Action Research' the third section (rather than the first, as is the case in many such texts), following discussions of the conceptual underpinning, and the validity of action research, provides a refreshing and useful backdrop to the practice-based issues involved in doing this type of research.

 Additional online resources can be found at:
www.sagepub.co.uk/beraseries.sp

CHAPTER 2

GETTING TO GRIPS WITH PERSPECTIVES AND MODELS

Before starting any piece of research, it is important to identify clearly just what the purpose of that research is. It is only when this is done, that decisions about an appropriate methodological approach can be made. As suggested in Chapter 1, methodology is a term which requires some unpicking, particularly in relation to action research. For many novice researchers, there is a degree of confusion and conflation between the terms methodology and method. It is important first to distinguish between them, so that their usage is clearly understood by all. Methodology is the broader of the two terms, and can be thought of as a branch of logic, concerned with the principles behind knowledge construction. Method indicates the ways in which this knowledge construction process can be designed and asks what are the tools of the investigation that can assist with this? Action research is therefore a methodology, a way of understanding and generating knowledge about the complexities of practice. Models and schematics are ways in which we try to illustrate and articulate the concept, and can help in choosing appropriate tools or methods through which to engage in the process. This chapter will explore, first, some philosophical perspectives on action research, discussing its appropriateness for generating practice-knowledge, and discussing some of the conceptual matters facing action researchers in a way which, in the words of Bridges (2003), allows us to become philosophers in the classroom. Secondly, the chapter will consider some of the ways in which action research can be represented, understood and put into practice.

Perspectives: A little background philosophy

Carr in his 2006 paper asks 'What is methodology?' and 'What purpose does it serve?'. If we set Carr's questions in the context of Stenhouse's (1975) work on curriculum development, then we begin to get an idea in general terms, of how to go about addressing these questions. Stenhouse (1975), believing that curriculum development could only properly happen through teacher professional development, suggests that research contributes to the development of knowledge through systematic 'self-critical' enquiry, and that, 'research is systematic and sustained enquiry' made public. When the enquiry is rooted in practice, the question may take on a different tone given the complexity of educational practice. Indeed, Winter et al in 2000, ask just how can the intellectual qualities of workplace practice be identified, evidenced and assessed?. While this chapter will not focus on the assessing of such evidence, it will explore its nature, generation and place in an action research project. Undertaking practice-based research, which for many teachers is an essential part of postgraduate education programmes, provides an ideal opportunity to investigate this very issue. Further, it can illustrate and explore the essential theory–practice relationship evident in educational practice, which, in the words of Campbell and Groundwater-Smith, is a form of practice that crosses 'the boundaries between theory and practice where it creates praxis, the synthesis of theory and practice' (2010: 12). The concept of 'praxis' is an important one, which warrants further exploration.

I will attempt to draw on some of Wilf Carr's work in relation to methodology and action research, exploring the Aristotelian concepts of poiesis and praxis in order to illustrate something of the relationship between praxis and action research. The difference between these two forms of human action lies, Carr claims, in the moral nature of praxis, claiming that the 'end of praxis is not to make or produce some object or artefact, but progressively to realise the idea of the "good" constitutive of a morally worthwhile form of human life.' (2006: 426). In progressively working towards the good, praxis is therefore, he claims, a 'doing' form of action, rather than the more instrumental, 'making' poesis. Praxis thus is understood as a form of process, through which the end is realised through *interpretation in context*. It can, indeed, have no pre-specified outcome. As Bernstein suggests, 'In praxis there can be no prior knowledge of the right means by which we realize the end in a particular situation. For the end itself is only specified in deliberating about the means appropriate to a particular situation' (1983: 147).

Doing the right thing

A key concept embedded in this is the notion that the reasoning of praxis is symbiotic with the actions of a practitioner. As such therefore, it not the application of theory or reason to practice, it is the theorising of practice in context. Indeed, for MacIntyre (1981: 141), such reasoning, or phronesis, is a moral consciousness, leading practitioners to do 'the right thing in the right place at the right time in the right way'.

Carr (2007) identifies that educational research, as a practical science, needs to meet both epistemic and practice-based criteria, 'simultaneously contributing to the development of educational knowledge and to the improvement of educational policy and practice'. Given the dialogic relationship between theory and practice, between reason and action, and the developing understanding that evolves between them in a search to improve practice, it is interesting to note Malpas et al.'s (2002) comment on Gadamer's (1975) hermeneutics as a philosophy which cannot be founded on a particular method or set of rules. Gadamer does not denigrate the role of methodology, but rather, cautions about its limited role when seeking understanding of practical, situated activities. Conversation and dialogue are seen as key mechanisms through which such understandings can develop. As Carr (2005) suggests, in his keymore address to the CARN conference the fundamental function of such research is 'to keep the conversation going'.

I find myself agreeing with Carr's questions in relation to methodology and believe that, rather than getting tangled in discussion and debate about approaches to and forms of research, our primary focus should be the need to ensure that whatever approach we take to action research, it should be a conversational rather than an operational one. For the novice researcher, however, some sort of schematic representation that supports such a conversational approach is vital. Engaging in a conversation with practice in a way that is neither bounded nor guided allows opponents of action research to decry its lack of intellectual rigour. The considered and nuanced use of models of action research allows the process to be both conversational and supported by a rigorous intellectual framework.

Drawing on Stenhouse's (1975) notion of the need to make the products of research (which is a systematic and sustained process) public, we immediately begin to see how a practitioner's normal reflection-in-action is not such a systematic or sustained process. It is an 'in the minute' demonstration of the tacit professional knowledge of the practitioner. Action research, on the other hand, is the product of planned deliberation, of systematic data collection, collation and analysis, of theory testing and theory generation, and adheres to some agreed principles. Its results may be disseminated orally, in written reports or in other ways which will be discussed in Chapter 8. Crucially, they should also be subjected to the discussion and debate of scholars and practitioners in the field.

For most action researchers in schools and other educational settings, the improvement of practice rather than policy is the central focus. Practice improvement may also seem to be more important to teachers than development of educational knowledge. However, this might suggest that educational knowledge is an abstract thing, couched in language and concepts foreign to the classroom, residing only in books and scholarly articles. McAteer and Dewhurst (2010: 34) touch on the nature of educational knowledge in school contexts, suggesting that action research has a very specific purpose, 'enabling professionals to understand their practice better, and use that enhanced understanding in order to effect changes in practice'. It is in this understanding of practice that 'educational knowledge' resides. Through understanding practice in a deeply considered and examined way, teachers develop highly contextualised educational knowledge which not only can provide a basis for the development of an appropriate conceptual framework, but also can become an analytic device. In developing a deep and sophisticated understanding of their own professional contexts, teachers become more adept at understanding other contexts, and the overarching educational policy agenda.

The intricate and reciprocal relationship between theory and practice is a concept which is usually very familiar to most teachers. In developing the skills of teaching, teachers quickly recognise the significance (and the actuality) of those times when Schön's (1983) notion of 'reflection-in-action' is a key element of their practice. This ability to both theorise and 'do' educational practice, this conversation between practice and theory, is one key difference between the experienced and the inexperienced educator. The responsiveness of the more experienced practitioner to the classroom dynamic, to unspoken learner feedback, allows a teacher to conduct an on-the-spot analysis of the evidence presented to them, and almost instantly, translate that into a changed and more appropriate action. On a small scale, this emulates the action research process in that it is both a theoretical and a practical activity. In the more developed action research approach, Winter's 'intimate and principled linkage' (1987: 21) is an ongoing conversation between research and action, between practice and theory.

This 'intimate and principled linkage' has been conceptualised by many theorists (for example, Carr and Kemmis, 1986; Elliott, 1981, 1991) as a methodological approach characterised by right or moral judgement, and underpinned by democratic principles, acknowledging and recognising evidence from practice, and contributing to a theorising, or theory-generative approach, rather than subjecting practice to the application of theory.

How then might we go about translating the reflection-in-action of a skilled practitioner into action research? How can we 'keep the conversation going' in an academically defensible way? If such conversation is the function of action research, what then is its form?

Representations of action research

All models of action research are deeply rooted in the notion of reflection – again an often used, but loosely defined, word. It is helpful, therefore, to begin by considering the nature of professional and critical reflection.

Reflection

While the word 'reflection' does not feature often in the UK Professional Standards for Teachers (tda.gov.uk), it appears twice in the standards for achieving Qualified Teacher Status (QTS) where trainee teachers are exhorted to 'Reflect on and improve their practice' (Q7) and 'Support and guide learners to reflect on their learning' (Q28), with the second of these statements being repeated in the core professional standards (C33). It is clear, though, that there is an expectation that teachers will engage in reflection about their practice, with full sections in the QTS, Core and Excellent Standards being devoted to '*reviewing* teaching and learning'.

It is helpful therefore to consider the normal day-to-day reflection that is embedded in a teacher's practice, and consider its relation to the more critically reflective practice that is required on postgraduate programmes, and which forms a lynchpin of the action research process. For many teachers, day-to-day reflection involves reviewing the effectiveness of delivering a set of learning outcomes, of engaging learners in formative feedback activities and ensuring that a range of pedagogies is used to support the diverse needs of learners. While these are necessary and commendable activities, action research is predicated on the concept of a more critically reflective practice, which challenges the teacher to move beyond the 'normal' evaluation of practice to a more problematising approach; one which raises questions, and seeks alternative perspectives. The action research models and representations presented later in this chapter are all predicated on critically reflective practice as their starting point and, as

such, the quality of this foundational reflection is of paramount importance. Indeed, since initial reflection may generate a substantial part of the
initial data, its quality could be considered vital to the success, or otherwise, of the project. For many practitioners, keeping a reflective diary or
log is one way of capturing these reflections. Bolton (2005: 166) suggests
that those who write learning journals 'take responsibility for discovering
personal learning needs' and 'question, explore, analyse personal experience'. Moon (2006) suggests that such journals support metacognition,
thus enabling their writers to learn about their own learning.

Frameworks for reflection

A number of writers provide frameworks for reflection, with that of
Ghaye and Ghaye (1998), still valuable in its five-part typology. They
suggest that reflection on practice should be:

1 Descriptive, in that it is personal and retrospective.
2 Perceptive, in that it has an emotional aspect.
3 Receptive, in that it relates personal views to those of others.
4 Interactive, in that it links learning to future action.
5 Critical, in that it places the individual teacher within a broader 'system'.

For many action researchers, a framework of this type can support the early
and ongoing reflections that are an integral part of the project itself. It can
most usefully be incorporated into the research diary which can be used
throughout a project as 'a space in which to become initially analytic, spot
emergent themes and theoretical insights' (McAteer, 2012: 191). In this way
the diary can simultaneously provide a history of the project, the initial and
later analyses, and the questions that arise for the researcher along the way.
    Chapter 4 develops the notion of critical reflection on practice as a
source of data for a project.

Representations of action research

A concern for improvement in educational practice is often what first brings
education practitioners into action research programmes. For some this
may be the main purpose, with the 'academic' part being simply there as
added value. The desire to make some improvement in practice, to solve
some problem or, indeed, pose some problem may be the key driver. For
many, there is an expectation that university-based professional development programmes will provide answers to concerns in practice. Teachers
often register for such programmes hoping that they will be taught new

and better ways of doing, and can initially find it both frustrating and challenging to be told that there is no quick-fix solution on offer. Instead, they may find that they are told to reflect on their own situation, keep diaries, ask questions and, on the basis of this, find a way of making sense within their own practice and context, and hence attempt to improve it. Having hoped for some external solution to their concerns, they are sent back to the very heart of their concerns. In the words of Popper:

> We start, I say, with a problem, a difficulty. It may be practical or theoretical. Whatever it may be when we first encounter the problem we cannot, obviously know much about it. At best, we have only a vague idea what our problem really consists of. How then can we produce an adequate solution? Obviously we cannot. We must first get better acquainted with the problem. (1972: 260)

Although not writing about action research, Popper captures much of its essence. Without adequately knowing our problem, how can we ensure that any solution is appropriate?

The first step, therefore, for the aspiring action researcher is to get to know the problem. It is here that the use of an appropriate roadmap or schematic comes into its own. At this stage in the process, the novice researcher sees this schematic as a governing recipe or procedure. Initially, this is comforting and, of course, throughout the process, it is a useful aid in maintaining the academic integrity of the endeavour and enabling the process to be conducted in such a way as to be communicable to others. McTaggart (1996: 248), however, cautions against the belief that following the chosen algorithm is the same as 'doing action research', adding that 'action research is not a "method" or a "procedure" for research but a series of commitments to observe and problematise through practice a series of principles for conducting social enquiry'. The researcher must be careful therefore to avoid what Hammersley (2006: 276) calls 'methodology-as-technique', but instead, strive for the approach he calls 'methodology-as-philosophy', which 'highlights the role of philosophical assumptions in research'.

What then might action research 'look like'? What representations can help novices get to grips with the doing of it, and its underpinning conversational philosophy? At a basic level, it has some key characteristics that I have touched on:

• It is a practice-based approach.
• It incorporates and builds on critical reflection on practice.
• It is driven by a desire to improve (personal) practice.
• It can contribute to the development of professional knowledge.

Exploration of some of the models of action research also reveals that:

- It is an iterative process, each cycle being subject to review and reflection.
- It is intellectually and epistemologically defensible.

The next section of the chapter discusses these issues in relation to some common models of action research.

Getting to know the problem, trying to find a solution

In getting started on an action research project, the practitioner must first ensure that the question being asked is suited to this methodological approach, and must then decide just how they will make their work intellectually sound and rigorous. Many guidelines exist to help practitioners formulate an appropriate question, but in summary they incorporate the following key pointers:

- It should (usually) relate to improving your own practice – 'how can I improve what I do in relation to . . . ?'.
- It should allow you to develop explanations, hypotheses and relate them to a wider theoretical base.
- It should be rooted in something that is within your locus of control, both in terms of access to the field and data, and also in relation to the potential for action.
- It should have personal and professional importance, and allow you to deepen knowledge and understanding, while still being of interest, and indeed relevance, to others in the field.

In my experience of supervising students on action research projects, it is only when they have actually clarified the research focus that they can begin to understand what trajectory their project might take, and hence make choices in terms of frameworks or approaches.

It is also perhaps pertinent at this stage to introduce a cautionary note. The teacher in a classroom, the school leader, or the practitioner in any other setting may be faced with a number of aims in undertaking practice-based research. In the current climate these may be competing aims. When professional development programmes are funded in part or in total by schools, participants may find themselves under pressure to complete projects which have been decided by senior staff in the school. It is sometimes the case that these projects are expected to evaluate some initiative which has been introduced. Perhaps a school has introduced a new timetable structure, and the head wishes to know if it has been effective (as hoped), in reducing incidents of unacceptable behaviour. New curriculum initiatives often form part of school improvement plans, and as such, leadership teams (rightly) would like to have some means of evaluating their success. While such projects may produce some useful information in relation to the effectiveness of the strategies in meeting hoped-for ends, they usually generate relatively little understanding or theorising of practice. Reflecting on the features of action research questions, such projects clearly do not fit this remit. (We pick up on this point in Chapter 3.) This is not to say that such projects are of lower worth or significance than action research projects; it is simply a statement of their difference, and a word of caution to prevent misconceptualising them.

Finding a suitable action research model

Once a practitioner has decided that a question is of the action research type (in that it incorporates the essence of the features listed above), the next step is to decide how exactly the research project will be designed. Many representations of the action research process exist and, for the novice action researcher, navigating the field can be fraught with challenges. The tendency in some circles for any practitioner research to be called 'action research' can further compound this. While this can at one level, make the approach seem accessible to teachers and other practitioners, such misuse of the term does much damage to both the quality of output and the public perception of action research.

From this perspective, then, it is important that those undertaking action research projects do so with due regard for the academic rigour and integrity of their undertakings. The 'Plan–Act–Reflect' cycle often promoted through in-service courses for practising teachers owes its origins to the 1981 Kemmis and McTaggart model which encouraged a four-step approach, introducing the element of 'observe', often illustrated in a similar way to the representation in Figure 2.1.

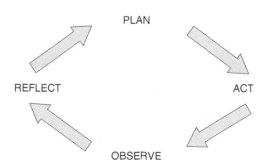

Figure 2.1   The Plan-Act-Observe-Reflect cycle

Carr and Kemmis further developed this approach in 1986 to indicate the cyclic nature of action research, the outcomes of each cycle informing the development of the next. Riding et al. (1995), and most writers since, represent it as a series of cycles each feeding into and informing the next, thus identifying it as an iterative process as in Figure 2.2.

McNiff (2002) produces a less 'tidy', though some would say more realistic, graphical representation, showing a spiral increasing in diameter and spawning other spirals along the way. In this way, she captures effectively the messiness of action research. Her model recognises and illustrates the process as evolving, changing in focus and, in the words of Mellor (2001) and Cook (1998), 'messy'. This 'messiness' is both a strength and a challenge in action research. A particular strength is in its authentic description of the process, which in itself can provide practitioners with the assurance of knowing that their project, in being 'messy', has not necessarily 'gone wrong'. However, the model of accountability in which education currently finds itself is suggestive of positivistic modes of thinking, desire for 'proof', replicability, objectivity and measurability. There is an implied concept of linearity and predictability in terms of the type of research that might be done, and anything deviating from that mode may be seen as undesirable. For those undertaking classroom or practice-based research, this can create a significant tension in that more positivistic or scientific approaches can very quickly prove ill matched to the research in question. Messiness, however, causes uncertainty and, as such, can be unnerving during an action research project. McNiff's model, while initially challenging and perhaps best understood from inside the messiness of action research, does, I feel, provide a sense of security for those finding themselves in their first experience of 'messy' research. Seeing her apparently untidy model can help the novice researcher feel less unsettled by the unpredictability of his or her own research process. This issue of messiness is discussed in more detail in Chapter 7.

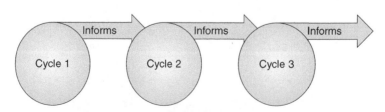

Figure 2.2   The cyclic nature of action research

Elliott (1991) provides a more structured schematic than those identified above, and while its tidiness and apparent linearity may seem at
odds with the messiness of the action research process, it is this very
tidiness and structural linearity that makes it such a useful representation
for many beginning action researchers. It takes as a starting point the
outline model shown in Figure 2.2, fleshing it out with description of the
various stages within each cycle. The way in which the cycle is
unpicked and narrated is found by many to be both pragmatically and
conceptually helpful. Presented as a flow chart (Elliott, 1991: 71), taking the research from an 'initial idea' through 'reconnaissance', 'general
plan' and 'action steps', to the monitoring and evaluating of the implementation, it can provide a comforting sense of solidity and predictability at the start of a project. In my experience, many students like this
model to guide them on their first encounter with action research, and
only when they have begun to feel more comfortable with the inevitable
uncertainty can they see the value in other more 'untidy' representations.
The particular appeal that this model holds for me is in its simplicity and
explanatory layout. A big challenge faced by most novice action
researchers is in allowing the early stage of the project to be data driven.
The temptation to jump to conclusions about the possible 'cause' of
some phenomenon, the desire to see what the literature says in relation
to it, or just the dominance of a current discourse blunting sensitivity to
other, possibly more important, messages from the initial data set, are all
potential pitfalls which this schematic can help researchers navigate.

A simplified version of action research schema that I have found helpful
in mentoring and supporting new researchers is presented as a template
in Table 2.1, outlining key actions at each stage in a single cycle, with
some exemplification as to what those questions might mean in a practice-
based situation. It is deliberately 'practical' in its articulation, and is not
intended as an alternative for the deep thought and discussion that will go
into developing and undertaking an action research project. It is, however,
a useful hook for these discussions at tutorials/supervision meetings and
can help a new researcher see inside an action research cycle.

Whichever model or schematic is chosen is very much personal
choice. They all advocate a cyclic, iterative process of research where the
initial focus of the research is subject to ongoing review and reflection
through the repetition of plan, act, observe and reflect cycles. As a process, this recurrent refining and reformulation is well suited to the
dynamic and complex nature of the human interactions that occur in
educational practice. It is, in fact, the development and more explicit
articulation of Schön's (1983) 'reflection-in-action' with the addition of
'reflection-on-action'.

Table 2.1 Inside an action research cycle

Stage	Action
1	**Starting off, and clarifying a research question** Your school/setting has decided to do a review of its teaching and learning policy. This makes you think about the way in which you teach your students, and about how well they learn in your class. You wonder if they are actually learning for understanding, or if it is more rote learning. You suspect that there is a lot of rote learning (one or two things students said in class recently make you think that), and would prefer if you could teach for deeper understanding. The initial research question that you formulate is: **'How can I change the way I teach my year 11 class, so that I help my students develop deeper understanding of history?'**
2	**What is the situation at present? And how can I find out?** This stage involves you undertaking an exploration of your own practice (the reconnaissance phase). You might decide to keep a reflective diary focusing on your teaching of the class. You might also decide to have a class/focus group discussion, in order to canvas student views, look at samples of student work for evidence of their rote learning. Alternatively, or additionally, you might issue a questionnaire, engage the help of a critical friend to observe your lessons – there are lots of ways you might gather evidence about the present state of play, and lots of sources of that evidence. These will contribute to the initial evidence which you analyse to see if there are any key issues arising from it. You then try to understand these issues by looking at some relevant reading materials.
3	**What changes can I make? Action steps** Using the initial analysis from stage 2, you start to develop some strategies to address the issues which the evidence has identified. This becomes an action plan which you implement over a period of time, and monitor. During the implementation phase, you collect evidence – much as before – to inform you as to whether or not the changes are having the desired effect.
4	**Evaluate the effect of these changes** After you have collected, collated and analysed the evidence from stage 3, once again, you can read around the issues arising in your findings, and attempt to then evaluate whether your strategies have worked, to what extent and, more importantly, try to gain an understanding of WHY. It is also important – sometimes MORE important – to explain any 'failures'.
5	**Revisiting the original research question in the light of your findings** Action research is a cyclic process and, so, after each action step, you revisit the original research question, assess the extent to which you have been able to address it, and evaluate what has been done. It is normal practice to then refine the question (your focus will have sharpened by this stage) and repeat the cycle of action step/reflection.

Stage	Action
	You can see that this could go on for quite some time! Most people design their projects within the constraints of time and other resources available, and perhaps run simply two cycles of the action research process. In a shorter project, it may just be one full cycle. Each cycle, however, should further develop your understanding and refine your question, until you are coming closer to a resolution.

When will you do all this?
This needs to be realistic, and realisable. Take into account predictable interruptions, such as school concerts, examinations and other family/personal events that may disrupt your research. Plan your time to take account of these, and build in the flexibility to cope with the inevitable, but unexpected, interruptions.

It's all about me

Having clarified a research focus, and found an action research model that seems to suit, many novice researchers are still unsettled by their own centrality in the process and their perception that it will produce subjective, and therefore invalid, research.

Initial tutorials with tutors or discussions with peers often incorporate proposals to ensure that the research is objective, and hence 'valid'. Most of us have at some time offered a provisional analysis of a situation, preceded with 'I know I'm not being very objective here, but . . . '. In some way, we offer this as an apology for the perceived poor quality of what is to follow. The early stages of an action research project are particularly susceptible to this mindset.

However, it must be remembered that a particular strength in action research is the acknowledged location of the practitioner right at the heart of the process. In being constructed like this, in having 'I' at the core of the action research question, it is deeply personal and contextualised, drawing on the values and beliefs of the researcher, and challenging him/her to reconcile those values and beliefs with practice. It immediately provides a challenge to the often sought objectivity that seems to characterise 'good' research. Throughout this book the power of the 'dominant discourse' will be discussed in one way or another. This search for the perceived validity of objectivity is one such trigger point. No matter what our educational discipline, we live in an increasingly scientistic society, where quality criteria for almost everything from cat food to teaching are predicated on a set of numeric indicators or metrics. Office for Standards in Education (OFSTED) lesson observations are scored on a scale of 1 to 4, while the superior quality of some brands of cat food is advertised on the basis of the preference of 8 out of 10 cats. It is this mindset, this predisposition to (the dominant) notions of quantifiability and objectivity that we bring to our engagement with action research. For many teachers, this can be a most troublesome aspect of the process.

In the initial reconnaissance phase of an action research project the ways in which the researcher goes about collecting, collating and analysing early data from the field are fundamental in getting the project off to a good start. The recognition and acknowledgement of personal values and the propensity for bias are key attributes for the researcher at any stage in a project, but particularly so at the start when we are still so used to working in a more scientific mindset. It is helpful, therefore, to explore in more detail the nature of the first stages of an action research cycle. The initial fact-finding, or reconnaissance phase, coupled with early analysis is what will guide and support the rest of the project, and getting it right, or at least not wrong, is both challenging and rewarding. Key 'skills' in this respect are, first, a sensitivity to the data themselves and, secondly, a clear and explicit recognition of the place and role of personal values in action research.

Sensitivity

First, I briefly discuss what I mean by sensitivity to the data. As teachers we are accustomed to observing what is happening in our own and other classrooms. In many ways, we have become quite expert at it, and it is this sensitisation to classroom observation that enables us to become adept at reflection-in-action. We have effectively internalised criteria for observing and assessing practice, and can apply them almost unthinkingly. It is this very expertise, though, that may become a stumbling block at the start of an action research project. In the initial reconnaissance phase, the practitioner needs to almost suspend this agenda, and become open to noting the unexpected, that which does not fit in with standard observational criteria, and indeed, that which may not initially seem to be significant in terms of the focus of the research. Mason (2002: xi) describes this as a form of professional sensitivity:

> As a professional, you are sensitised to notice certain things in professional situations. To develop your practice means to increase the range and decrease the grain size of relevant things you notice, all in order to make informed choices as to how to act in the moment, how to respond to situations as they arise

This sensitisation to the unexpected, to the seemingly insignificant, contributes significantly to the quality of the analysis and, hence, to the quality of and justification for any subsequent action. Later chapters will explore ways in which this can be helped to happen, and the problems that can occur when it does not. At this stage, however, only a brief pointer is appropriate.

Personal values

The second of the key 'skills' I mention, which relates to personal values and their role and place in action research, is perhaps an even more important, and probably a more conceptually difficult, 'skill' to acquire. When objectivity is understood to be the key quality indicator in research (and the use of randomised control tests is commonly held as the gold standard in research), the place of personal value and belief can be difficult to understand. In addition, to adopt an entirely differing, and to some extent oppositional paradigmatic stance is in itself a major challenge, McAteer et al., drawing on the work of Backfield (1995), suggest that: 'Paradigmatic assumptions, are . . . the hardest for us to challenge, as they represent the way in which we have learned to see and understand the world. Most of us are highly resistant to such challenges . . .' (2010: 19).

But is it objective?

It is important to introduce some thoughts about the possibility of objectivity, something that will emerge again as discussion points in later chapters.

Crotty (1998) suggests that objectivism is a knowledge system which is in contrast to the subjective knowledge system deriving from opinion, belief, assumptions and feelings. It is thus a knowledge system in which these have no part and, as such, is claimed by its advocates to be value neutral. It is this objective, value-neutral status which renders it relatively immune to attack. Smith suggests that research (which he defines as an enquiry that yields systematic explanation) must set aside human attributes such as emotion, values and feelings:

> In order to develop systematic explanation, inquiry must be pursued in a way that holds at bay the normally pressing concerns and desires and values of the individuals involved. Again, in its most generalised sense, this means setting aside the typically human or anthropocentric approach to experience. (1963: 113)

In other words, research should, according to Smith, be conducted objectively. In relation to practice-based research, and action research in particular where the focus is on me and the improvement of my practice, I have real difficulty in setting aside an anthropocentric response to my personal experiences. The fact that it may seem an unreasonable response, or outside the perceived normal range, may be interesting to explore, but it does not, nor should not, invalidate my response. In my experience, this is something experienced by most, if not all, action researchers.

Philosophical problems arise when considering the objective, or depersonalised, nature of knowledge, particularly that which is practice derived or experiential. Even when we consider science, traditionally viewed as a highly objective form of knowledge, history provides us with many and telling examples that suggest otherwise. There are accounts of the selective use of experimental data in order to support a predetermined thesis. (see Broad and Wade, 1985; Milton, 1994; Sheldrake, 1994; and Swartz, 1992, for a fuller description and discussion). In each case, scientists have either deliberately chosen only confirmatory data from the full set (in the famous Millikan Oil Drop experiment, the results of which informed much of what we now know and understand as contemporary chemistry and physics, only 42 per cent of the data were used!), or undertaken a manipulative technique known as data reduction in which compensations are made to a data set to adjust it for the effects of contingent factors, in order to produce confirmatory data. In each case, it would be hard to claim that the 'normally pressing concerns and desires and values of the individuals involved' (Smith, 1963: 113) have been held at bay.

Views such as these illustrate the extent to which the theory dependence of data analysis calls into question the assumed objectivity of scientific data. The extent to which observations are theory laden is also often the extent to which it is value laden. By this I mean that discarded data which are deemed wrong because they do not verify the initial theory, are also deemed inferior in quality, of a lower (if any) value. The judgement of what constitutes good data, and what should be discounted as anomalous/fluke data is made primarily on a subjective rather than an objective basis. There is usually no set of objective criteria for making this judgement other than the fact that the results deviate from the expected.

Returning to educational practice, and even setting aside philosophical and epistemological concerns, I believe it would be hard to convince any practitioner that his or her school-based practice or research should set aside Smith's 'normally pressing concerns and desires and values of the individuals involved', or the 'typically human or anthropocentric approach to experience'. Given that many teachers base their teaching on experiential learning approaches, and acknowledge the importance of the attitudinal and affective responses to these approaches, it would be difficult to imagine them describing knowledge of and in the classroom as objective, value free and not strongly bound up in the individuals involved. How should we begin to understand our role as educators were we to dehumanise it?

Let us now explore the 'human' face of researching practice. It seems clear from these early explorations in relation to action research that practice is complex, challenging, sometimes confusing and rarely, if ever, predictable. As such, action research must not only cope with that but, given the intimate theory–practice link which it epitomises, must demonstrate similar properties and behaviours.

The dynamic nature of action research: some more about uncertainty

I referred earlier in the chapter to the importance of the initial reconnaissance phase of action research. This, in effect, builds the foundation for the rest of the project, both analytically and in terms of project design. Initial data analysis will impact on the subsequent cycle, will set up an orientation to a particular theoretical framework and, therefore, potentially directly inform the outcome of later cycles. It is possible also, even likely, that analysis of data at the reconnaissance phase will result in some degree of revision to the initial research design. The need for a particular type of data might suggest a more image-based data collection tool than had been previously considered. A different perspective may be felt necessary in light of the initial analysis. Conversely, a deeper probing into an existing data set may be indicated. Whatever the reasons, one thing is clear: action research can take a different trajectory to that first imagined or planned. As such, it is a dynamic and responsive approach.

Earlier in this chapter, I introduced the notion that the representation of action research as a flow chart or other schematic, no matter how 'untidy', may be suggestive of a route that is mapped out at the start. Similarly, McNiff's model has a self-evident dynamic sense to it, but it may still be difficult for the novice researcher to see it as such, and forays into the unexpected can still prove unnerving. Cook (1998, 2009) talks of the importance of mess in action research, and its purpose in developing rigour. Likewise, Mellor (2001: 478) discusses how he 'may wish to draw on a range of techniques and ideas in dealing with the messy reality of my research practice'. Describing the tensions between academic rigour and readability in practitioner research, he presents a narrative that will ring true for many action researchers. Citing Cornett (1995), Mellor argues

that 'doubt and uncertainty are the fuel that drives . . . research' (p. 123) and
that it is 'refreshing to find thoughtful writings . . . that vividly portray the intellectual and emotional struggles that researchers face when they are truly concerned about truth value and ethical behaviour in their work' (p. 123), although
'it is rare that authors share their angst publicly' (p. 123) (Mellor, 2001: 478)

thus illustrating with clarity the challenges involved in both doing and
writing action research. Chapter 7 picks up the matter of writing up
action research projects.

Inventiveness, creativity and living theory

In relation to 'doing' action research, Marion Dadds's works on methodological creativity and inventiveness (Dadds, 1995; Dadds and Hart,
2001) are key texts for any aspiring action researcher faced with the
messiness, complexity and constraints of undertaking action research.
Not only do they provide comfort to the action researcher struggling
with such issues, but they legitimate the possibilities of methodologically
creative or inventive responses to these situations.

> More important than adhering to any specific methodological approach,
> be it that of traditional social science or traditional action research, may
> be the willingness and courage of practitioners – and those who support
> them – to create enquiry approaches that enable new, valid understand-
> ings to develop; understandings that empower practitioners to improve
> their work for the beneficiaries in their care. Practitioner research meth-
> odologies are with us to serve professional practices. So what genuinely
> matters are the purposes of practice which the research seeks to serve,
> and the integrity with which the practitioner researcher makes method-
> ological choices about ways of achieving those purposes. (Dadds and
> Hart, 2001: 169)

They also provide us with strong links to the 'teacher self-study' and 'living theory' approaches to practitioner research. Arguably, teacher self-
study does not have the implicit 'action' imperative that characterises
action research, but the movement towards such reflective and reflexive
approaches, championed by Tom Russell and others, contributes much
of value to action researchers. Wood (2010: 105) uses self study to
'attempt to demonstrate how values-based, self-study action research can
help provide answers to questions about educational theory'.
  Likewise, living theory allows the practitioner to generate a unique,
and uniquely valid understanding about their own lived experiences of
practice, but also contains an imperative to action. In the words of Jack
Whitehead on the front of his website.

In a living educational theory approach to action research, individuals hold their lives to account by producing explanations of their educational influences in their own learning in enquiries of the kind, 'How am I improving what I am doing?' They do this in contexts where they are seeking to live the values they use to give life meaning and purpose as fully as they can. http://www.actionresearch.net/

No matter which approach to action research we take, no matter which schematic guides our endeavours, we will ultimately find ourselves faced with the importance of articulating and interrogating our values in practice. Pring (2000), when discussing educational practice, describes it as composed of many and complex transactions, all of which are informed by the values and beliefs of the teachers and learners.

Values in action research

The notion of action research as a moral or ethical practice has featured in the work of many authors, including Elliott (1996, 2000), Carr (1987) and Bridges (2003). Bridges, talking of the element of 'responsibility' in action research says that, in relation to the consequences of one's actions:

> To take responsibility for them requires that one knows what they are and how they result from one's actions – i.e. the empirical part of the enquiry. But this is not enough. In addition, one has to be satisfied that they satisfy the educational principles, the values, which are one's own measure of the worth of one's educational practice – i.e. the evaluative and philosophical part of the enquiry. (2003: 189)

He cites the work of Elliott (2000) and Carr (1987), outlining ways in which 'educationally worthwhile' is defined in terms of 'value-concepts' (Elliott, 2000), and that:

> enquiry into how to realise educational values in the practices of teaching and learning (enquiries into means) cannot be separated from philosophical enquiry into what these values mean and their implications for practice (enquiries into ends). It cannot be reduced to studies of the instrumental effectiveness of particular teaching and learning methods in the light of fixed, unambiguous and tangible/measurable ends. (Elliott, 2000: 82–3)

These authors bring us a clear articulation of the presence of, and more importantly, the need for the exploration of values in action research. Kemmis, referring to action research as 'practical reasoning', suggests that it draws on 'understandings about one's own and others' intentions, understandings, meanings, values and interests, and on one's own and others' reflexive, unfolding understandings of the situation in which one is practising at any given moment' (2005: 391).

It is perhaps in the exploration of and possible confrontation of the values inherent in practice that novice researchers face what may be for them a surprising emotional challenge. The role of emotions in research is more likely to be discussed in action research texts than those relating to other forms of practitioner research, and is rarely if ever explored as part of the research process in more positivistic research reports. It is not unusual to read accounts in action research journals, or the *Electronic Journal of Living Theories* (*EJOLTS*), which is particularly interested in publishing articles 'that connect a *flow of life-affirming energy with living values such as love, freedom, justice, compassion, courage, care and democratic evaluation*' (emphasis in original) (http://ejolts.net/) which expose the researcher's feelings of vulnerability, confusion, insecurity and so forth. In writing about these experiences and feelings, the action researcher in effect bares their soul. This is not an easy thing to do, is never undertaken lightly, and requires the caring supervision of an experienced and knowledgeable mentor or tutor.

Preparing to get started

How, then, should the novice action researcher approach the territory? It is my belief, supported by many years' experience of inducting people into action research, that having the appropriate mindset is as important as having a road map. A willingness to listen to the data with an open mind, to uncover, articulate and challenge assumption, to consistently question 'the way it is', and a preparedness for uncertainty, will be of more use than having a clear set of rules and procedures which could be applied with little understanding. While the importance of becoming familiar with the methodological literature cannot be underestimated, it does need to happen with an open and enquiring disposition which will acknowledge the possibility of finding other sources of support, and which sees the need for an eclectic, yet philosophically consistent, literature. Chapter 5 introduces some alternative perspectives on 'the literature' in action research, making a case for those texts which speak to the philosophical and substantive matters under consideration, those which happen upon us with seemingly little relevance at first, as well as the traditionally conceived body of appropriate literature.

Preparation for undertaking an action research project is vital. Too often, and particularly when it is part of an educational initiative project

rather than as part of award-bearing professional development programmes, training and support for the researcher is at best *ad hoc* and
at worst non-existent. Award-bearing programmes frequently provide
'research methods' courses prior to the final extended study or dissertation, and these can provide significant support and guidance for new
researchers. A range of guiding texts can all help beginning researchers,
but the support of an appropriate supervisor or other mentor (or in some
cases a community of critical friends) is essential both to the well-being
of the researcher and to the academic integrity of the project.

Further reading

Dadds, M. and Hart, S. (2001). *Doing Practitioner Research Differently.* London:
RoutledgeFalmer.

In coining the term 'methodological inventiveness', Dadds and Hart show
how academic integrity is not necessarily the preserve of highly structured
or prescriptive enquiry modes. Developed in response to their own work
with teachers conducting research on their practice, they were moved to
try to better understand the way in which teachers learn professionally,
and go about organising that learning. If you would like to see some of
the creative possibilities available to you, this book would provide an
accessible and enlightening introduction.

Elliott, J. (1991) *Action Research for Educational Change.* Milton Keynes: Open University
Press.

Although there have been many subsequent texts and papers published
by Elliott, this earlier work is still a key text in that it deals with the early
forays of school teachers into action research in the 1980s and early 1990s,
describing and discussing the dilemmas involved for practitioners and the
tensions involved in doing action research within a prescriptive curriculum framework. In addition, a sound section on models of action research
provides a useful structural schematic for novice action researchers.

Additional online resources can be found at:
www.sagepub.co.uk/beraseries.sp

SECTION 2

DOING ACTION RESEARCH

CHAPTER 3

GETTING STARTED ON AN ACTION RESEARCH PROJECT

This chapter explores and illustrates some very real concerns that teachers may have in undertaking an action research project. Attempts to demystify the research process, and to make educational inquiry an integral part of professional practice, have resulted to some extent in a dilution of meaning, particularly in relation to the term 'action research'. Used as a catch-all phrase to denote any form of reflective practice or practice-based enquiry, it has become common parlance in most schools and settings. Teachers encountering it as an acknowledged methodology during postgraduate study bring with them a comfortable familiarity with the term itself, but often a total lack of understanding of its underpinning epistemology. This can cause considerable difficulty in the early stages of a project, where one of the first tasks is to choose a methodology matched to the research question or focus.

The use of real examples in this chapter will help illustrate, and hopefully correct, some common misconceptions around action research, discuss valid starting points, and the ways in which effective reflection in and on practice is an integral part of the action research process. We follow the progress of Lauren as she finds a valid starting point for an action research project in her postgraduate professional development programme.

A case of mistaken identity

Lauren's story, part 1

Lauren is a teacher of five years' experience, who has been working in a secondary school which is consistently assessed as 'good' or better, by both internal evaluation processes and OFSTED inspections. The school is of medium size, set in an urban area, with a demographic that broadly reflects the national averages in terms of free school meal entitlement, English as an additional language, additional learning needs, and other comparable metrics. The headteacher provides effective leadership, and is open to exploring new initiatives in the ongoing quest for school improvement. Teachers feel well supported in their work, and the ethos of the school is one which in general supports open and free dialogue and discussion.

In the past year, Lauren has registered to do some postgraduate study, and hopes that in doing so she will be able to have a positive impact on her own teaching. Senior colleagues in the school have been supportive of her decision, as many of them have themselves seen the benefit of such programmes. Confident of the support she will receive in school, she is now about to begin a specialist action research module in which she will be required to undertake a piece of research, of her own design, within an action research methodological approach.

Following an internal school review, it had been agreed that the school should undertake a review of its social, personal and citizenship education provision at Key Stage 3. Lauren has always had a special interest in this aspect of education, and enjoys her role as a form tutor. She would like to use the opportunity afforded by her postgraduate course to help her develop and improve this aspect of her practice. Her headteacher has asked her if she would conduct an audit of current provision as her action research research assignment, and present a summary of it to the senior leadership team, in the hope that it will lead to an action plan being developed and implemented by the pastoral leader. Lauren prepares to present this as her project proposal to her university tutor.

Commentary

Like many students undertaking research projects as part of their postgraduate study, Lauren has found a focus for her work which fulfils some very important criteria. On the one hand, it relates to something she is particularly interested in and, on the other, it is a topic which will have the support of the senior leadership team in her school and will have the potential to have a positive impact on practice. She is aware that the best proposals for this type of research project exhibit these features of relevance, interest and support or permission. Additionally, she has heard of action research, and knows that it is often used as an approach which supports the improvement of practice. She goes to meet her tutor to discuss her action research proposal with a feeling of confidence and certainty.

Before we follow in her footsteps any more, it would be helpful to revisit and perhaps further develop an understanding of what is actually meant by the term 'action research', and think how that might help in getting started with a project.

Dick (2000) provides an elegantly simple definition: 'a family of research methodologies which pursue action and research outcomes at the same time'. He also suggests (like most other authors) that it is both reflective/reflexive, and cyclic in operation. Other descriptions and models of action research have been presented in Chapter 2, each showing the cyclic nature and the research/action relationship. This close relationship between research and action, between theory and practice, is more than just the use of research to make recommendations about practice, or the application of theory to practice, but depicts them as parts of a single whole. Campbell and Groundwater-Smith suggest that action research crosses 'the boundaries between theory and practice where it creates praxis, the synthesis of theory and practice' (Campbell and Groundwater-Smith (2010: 12).

This introduces the term 'praxis', a word from the Greek, which Carr (2005) favours in his descriptions, suggesting that action research is in essence a form of praxis, or 'practical philosophy'. This close relationship between theory and practice, between research and action brings two dimensions to the methodology. On the one hand, it outlines a particular epistemology which reframes the relationships between these dyadic pairs as dialogic rather than impositional. On the other hand, in introducing the centrality of the practitioner's own research, it starts to introduce a very personal dimension to this type of research. Returning to Elliott's (1978) suggestion that the focus of teacher action research should be identified by teachers themselves, it begins to become clear that a teacher action research project is essentially the formalisation of a teacher's (or other practitioner's) own desire to improve their own practice, by what could be described as a theorising approach to its exploration. Many authors including Carr, Bridges and Elliott emphasise the philosophical approach such an approach implies, the value-base of action research, and the moral nature and purpose of it. All of these questions bring us back to the matter of 'objectivity'. This conceptually large issue has already been highlighted in Chapter 2, and will continue to feature throughout the following chapters, but at this stage, it is perhaps appropriate to introduce the concept of 'declaring your hand', as Crotty (1998) would put it. Discussing the objectivity/subjectivity divide, he suggests that a constructionist view of knowledge, such as a practitioner-researcher often adopts, is one of meaning–making, and, as such, cannot be described simply as objective. He cautions us, however, that to adopt such a stance is to acknowledge that we then have a particular disposition towards the research itself, and towards the data and their interpretation. We cannot lose the 'self' and its impact in such a context. Cain (2011: 13) talks of the importance of understanding that 'the particular way in which teachers are positioned in classrooms affects their research methods'.

How do I improve my practice?

The work of Whitehead and McNiff in this regard is essential to take this discussion further. The concept of 'living theory' as action research has been a central theme in their work since the 1970s, and raises as a central question for action researchers, 'How do I improve my practice?' Together with McNiff, Whitehead uses this as a prompt for developing a framework that might guide practitioners through their research:

> We review our current practice,
>
> - identify an aspect that we want to investigate,
> - imagine a way forward,
> - try it out, and
> - take stock of what happens.
>
> We modify what we are doing in the light of what we have found, and continue working in this new way (try another option if the new way of working is not right).
>
> - monitor what we do,
> - review and evaluate the modified action,
> - and so on . . . http://jeanmcniff.com/ar-booklet.asp (3rd edn, 2002)

The extract above is taken from Jean McNiff's website, but variations on it appear frequently in her other work, Jack Whitehead's work and their joint work. All the frameworks challenge the practitioner to put themselves and their practice at the centre of the research. It is an approach which does not advocate research **on** practice, but research **as** practice and practice **as** research. This living theory approach neatly helps identify the key components to consider at the start of an action research project, and might usefully inform Lauren's research plans:

- Am I exploring something that I have identified, in my own practice, as something that I would like to understand better, and hence try to improve?
- Am I exploring something in my practice that I believe I ought to improve? Have I identified some example of where what I believe and what I do seem to be at odds?

- Have I identified a question that will allow me to engage with this type of theorising approach?
- Have I identified an area of my practice that I will have the power/authority to change?

Doing action research therefore makes us and our own concerns central to the research process itself. It is, therefore, a value-laden practice.

Reflection

Having read part 1 of the case study, and the subsequent commentary, reflect on the following questions:

- Is Lauren exploring something that she has identified, in her own practice, as something that she would like to understand better, and hence try to improve?

- Has Lauren identified a question that will allow her to engage with this type of theorising approach?

- Has Lauren identified an area of her practice that she will have the power/authority to change?

On the basis of your answers to the questions above, consider whether you think Lauren is proposing an action research project? Does her project challenge her to reflect on her own practice and its beliefs and values? Justify your answer.

Lauren's story, part 2

Lauren enthusiastically prepares for the meeting with her tutor. She has written an outline of her focus, identified some ways in which she might begin to audit current provision, and also, she has decided that she would like to interview a sample of staff and pupils in order to gain their perspectives on the relevance and effectiveness of the current programme. She has mapped out a time frame for the project, and has even tentatively approached some staff about the possibility of interviewing them. She is looking forward to getting started, and feels confident that her tutor will not only approve the project, but will commend the thoughtfulness of her approach to it, and the fact that she has made some initial enquiries to enable access to the field. In essence, she feels she has a sound project plan.

Her meeting with the tutor, however, does not go quite as expected, and Lauren is left feeling very deflated.

Reflection

Deliberate on the points below in relation to your previous reflections, and your own understanding of action research:

- What do you think might have 'gone wrong' at the meeting?
- What issues might her tutor have identified?

Commentary

Despite the best intentions of many practitioners, efforts to formulate and carry out action research projects can often result in something that represents a more technical, problem-solving research approach. In a culture where 'scientific' research is simultaneously misunderstood and yet culturally embedded, where the use of the word 'scientific' is used to mean 'without question', it is little wonder that we struggle conceptually with a research approach whose explicitly articulated standpoint is interpretive, grounded in complexity and uncertainty, and locates the researcher at both the centre of the practice and the research, designating them as a central and essential focus of the research rather than a contaminant. The notion that 'lack of objectivity' is not only acceptable but inevitable, is challenging, and one which is revisited in later chapters. Action research, as a problematising, problem-posing (rather than problem-solving) dialogic practice, draws on Frierean principles, and simultaneously acknowledges the reality and morality of complex social situations, while questioning and challenging our understanding of it.

The widespread (mis)use of the term is, in part, contributory to the situation Lauren, like many other practitioners, has found herself in. Having discussed her plans with senior colleagues in school, explaining that she was undertaking an action research module as part of her postgraduate course, she had been assured that this evaluation of the Social, Personal and Citizenship Education provision was indeed an action research project since it was practice-based. Further, she was assured that she would have access to all the information she would need, and staff would be made aware of her project, and encouraged to participate and assist where possible. The added bonus would be the possible impact of her findings on the school improvement plan, which, as her school had agreed to pay her course fees, seemed an appropriate return on their investment. Lauren herself would benefit if any of her recommendations were put in place by the pastoral leader on studying her findings and recommendations. It is interesting to note here that such misconceptions about the nature of an action research project can likewise be found in the 'academic' community. Kemmis (2007: 176) suggests that 'some of what passes for action research today is not action research at all but merely a species of field experimentation'. I would add to this that some is a species of initiative evaluation.

Reformulating a question

During the early negotiations, Lauren had found the arguments put forward by her senior colleagues to be very compelling, and in her limited understanding of the action research paradigm, felt that perhaps any initial uneasiness with their suggestions was due to her own misconceptions and misunderstanding. The meeting with her tutor, however, has now raised a separate concern for her. In addition to the feedback that he has given her indicating that her proposed study is actually an evaluation of the Social, Personal and Citizenship Education provision and not an exploration of her own practice and concerns in an effort to undertake cycles of reflection and revised action, she is beginning to wonder how she could undertake a 'proper' action research project, while still satisfying her senior leadership team that her work will benefit the school.

Lauren is, in a way, luckier than some beginning action researchers in that the headteacher has listened to her own area of interest and tried to help her find a way of doing something that lies within it. Other teachers may not be so lucky as they find themselves persuaded to take on projects which reflect needs and interests outside those which they would naturally choose. Negotiating a way through these potential conflict areas requires some sensitive discussion, and, I would argue, should be identified by course tutors as a real and pertinent concern for their teacher-students. The tensions between what teachers themselves want to do, and what school leaders might want them to do can cause unnecessary friction. Likewise, a misunderstanding of what action research can, and cannot, do, can be another source of friction and concern. A clear understanding of what action research is, and perhaps more importantly, is *not*, coupled with strategies for re-framing projects which do not meet the criteria for action research are important in the early stages of developing a focus or question for an action research project.

Reflection

Reflect now on the situation in which Lauren and her tutor find themselves, and consider the following:

- How might her tutor advise her on a way forward in this?
- What advice might he give her in relation to the formulation of her research question so that it is an appropriate one for an action research approach?
- What advice might he give her to help her in her discussions with the leadership team back at school?
- What texts would you recommend her to read at this stage?

The case of Lauren illustrates a particular dilemma in the initial stages of a project; that of having a ready framed question (often driven by a school (improvement) agenda) which is not methodologically suitable.

This search for an appropriate question and the misunderstanding of action research are widely reported concerns. Cain's (2011) paper 'Teachers' classroom-based action research' outlines the ways in which reports of small-scale studies indicate a lack of evidence in supporting the claims made. Citing a project completed by Rhodes in 2008, he illustrates clearly its lack of methodological and interpretive rigour, and ethical consideration. In fact, although described as 'action research', it was conducted on poorly designed quasi-experimental lines, which, despite the intention to undertake a comparative study, could not provide like-for-like participant groups, thus producing findings of questionable validity. The 'problem' with action research is widespread. In many cases it is still described and explained in terms that are contrary to its philosophy and epistemology. Oancea and Furlong (2007), having identified four key attributes of research (trustworthiness, contribution to knowledge, transparency and explicitness in design and reporting, and paradigmatic considerations), clearly explain the need to understand the paradigmatic considerations in which the research is taking place, saying:

> Finally we need to recognize that what is good research may well vary for any individual project on each of the above dimensions depending on the particular paradigm adopted – by 'paradigm' here we mean a complex of

epistemological/philosophical and methodological traditions, shared practices, etc, used within a particular 'epistemic community'. (Oancea and
Furlong, 2007: 128)

Let us now return to Lauren's story, and consider whether and how she
comes to terms with the paradigmatic considerations.

Lauren's story, part 3

Lauren's tutor, in advising her that what she was proposing was an evaluation of a school initiative, rather than a properly constructed action plan,
has left her feeling both demotivated and confused. She believes that her
research will result in making some recommendations which could translate
into practice. It is something that is important to her and, as such, she
initially begins to counter his feedback with a defence of her own position.
Surely this personal concern coupled with a possibility for later practice
development could be classed as action research? She argues that as she
will be doing the research (and some of it will involve her own responses to
the initiative) and that it might lead to some changes in practice, then it has
all the features of action research. It takes quite a long and difficult tutorial
to help her both clarify her misconception, and also find a way forward. At
the end, however, she feels that she has not only reaffirmed her understanding of action research, but also has a possible research focus which
she can bring back to her headteacher to discuss.

Commentary

Lauren is fortunate in that her tutor has a good understanding of the
context in which many of his students are carrying out their projects. He
immediately reassures Lauren that her misapprehension is understand-
able, and indeed not at all uncommon. Further, he suggests, there may
still be a way in which she can undertake a project that is close to her
own heart, but which might also resolve the issue of the project being
useful to her school leadership team.

In Lauren's case, the first thing her tutor considers is 'what is her
role in school, and on the basis of this, what type of action may be
possible for her'. This is the first thing that Lauren might think of
writing when she finally writes up her report. Her opening section
should introduce us to the project, the rationale for choosing it, and
a description of her role in relation to it. In doing this, Lauren will
not only help the reader (on coming to read the final report), but

will also clarify for herself both the possibilities and the limits of her proposed project. It can be a good starting point in relation to any initial ideas for a project to try to do this, and test it against one of the action research frameworks. Does your articulation of who you are and what you want to do 'fit' within an action research approach?

For Lauren, the discussion with her tutor about her own role in school was to become the most important one in helping get her back on track. Recognising that in her role as a form tutor she may be in a position to start to explore ways in which she can take stock of her current practice in relation to personal, social and citizenship education, and through that, devise ways in which to improve her practice, he suggests to her that in this way she could formulate an appropriate action research project based on her own practice. A question such as 'how can I better meet the personal, social and citizenship education needs of pupils in my form tutor group?' allows her to explore her own practice, the programme that she is using, and the pupils' perception of and attitudes towards it.

He suggests also, that her work could usefully inform the large key stage initiative previously discussed, as at the end of her project she will have completed a very detailed study into practice in one particular area of it. In addition to learning about her own practice, she will also have discovered important information about the programme itself and pupils' perspectives on it. In short, she will have generated a body of professional knowledge that will be of interest and use to herself and her colleagues.

In Chapter 6, we look at issues of applicability and relatability of action research findings, but at this stage it is sufficient to say that action research, like almost all practitioner research, makes no claims for generalisability or applicability, but instead, through providing deep insights into a particular instance, produces findings which can have relatability and resonance for other practitioners. Her findings, therefore, will raise questions for other practitioners in the area, which might guide them in questions about their own practice, or in a larger-scale programme review.

He also suggests to Lauren that, if it is possible within the context of her school setting, the project could be further enhanced (and made perhaps more meaningful to her leadership team) were she to undertake this collaboratively with one or more colleagues or even the pastoral leader. This provides Lauren with not only an acceptable focus for her project, but also a mechanism through which she can negotiate her changed focus with her school leadership team.

The importance of the context

As we reflect on Lauren's struggle to get started on her action research project, it is also germane to reflect on her tutor's role, particularly in relation to advising her how she might alter her focus, without losing the support of her school leadership team. This brings us to a seemingly minor, but extremely significant, aspect of action research proposals and reports (although we explore more fully in Chapter 7 some of the issues around reporting on action research projects). A description of the context in which the research is planned, the professional role and responsibilities of the researcher, and other matters, such as the demographic of the school or setting, the management structure and so forth, may all be vital elements in helping both the reader and, in the case of award-bearing programmes, the assessor, to understand not only the focus of the research and why it has been considered important, but also the nature of the practice that is being explored, and the possibilities and constraints on the researcher by virtue of their role. Many students I have worked with have experienced feedback on assignments and other assessed tasks which includes phrases such as 'your work would be improved by taking a more analytic approach' or similar. Anxious to ensure better performance in their next task, they focus on the analytic part of the report, and occasionally do so to the neglect of the descriptive part. As a reader, however, I find myself frustrated with reports that lack this initial description. Far from being the 'poor relation' in research reports, the initial description draws me into the narrative, and allows me to assess the appropriateness, or otherwise, of actions and decisions within the project. What is possible, and indeed appropriate, for a very senior member of staff in a school, may be entirely inappropriate (and unavailable as an action) to a very junior teacher. Likewise, the potential for collaboration is likely to be much greater in a large setting than in a very small one. Without the descriptive element though, decisions about these matters cannot easily be made.

The locus of the researcher's control

In the first part of the case study, we are introduced to Lauren's role. Knowledge of this is important for her tutor in helping her formulate her project proposal. Given the fundamental requirement to undertake action as part of the research (not as a possible follow-up to some fact-finding or evaluation process), it becomes clear that the nature of the intended project should be such that the associated action falls within the practitioner's locus of control. In other words, the person undertaking the project must be in a position and enabled or empowered to take action.

Let us consider some possible situations in which factors can affect the researcher's locus of control. There may be factors identified in the research which lie completely outside the scope of the practice context, regardless of management or other responsibilities. There may also be reasons of 'position' within a school or setting that mean certain courses of action are not available to the researcher. A question such as 'how can I improve the completion of homework for my year 8 pupils' is one which is limited in terms of potential for action for most teachers. While they can give homework tasks designed to engage and excite their pupils, if the root of the problem is a lack of home support or other external factor, then they are very much limited in terms of trying out well-targeted actions. It is almost certain that analysis of the data will suggest actions which reside outside the teacher's brief, or are completely beyond their remit and control. On the other hand, a question such as 'how can I make my classroom teaching more engaging for my year 8 pupils?' is located clearly within the teacher's locus of action (on the whole, but see below), and thus, it is likely that data analysis will suggest things that he or she is empowered to try out.

The extent to which a teacher or other practitioner is empowered to take particular courses of action will occasionally (though not always) depend on their position within a formal management structure. Change which is of a more systemic nature is not usually something which a more junior practitioner can easily undertake to implement or lead. In the example above about trying to make teaching more engaging for year 8 pupils, there may be some school-wide policies or directives about the structure of lessons or the resources that must be used. Taking action that would involve changing these whole-school practices would clearly be outside the teacher's locus of control. Some of those themes identified through data analysis may not be able to be undertaken as part of the project. In a situation like this, it is perfectly acceptable to explain why, despite there being five identified action steps, only the three that were possible in the particular context, were undertaken. The thinking-through of issues like this is an important part of getting started on action research.

Permissions

As is the case in any research plan, much forward thinking is needed in terms of how the project will be done, when and with whose involvement. Having established that the project is viable (in academic terms), there are other, more pragmatic considerations that must be dealt with at the early planning stage. Even before the project is designed in terms of data collection methods, researchers need to give some thought to the type of data they think they will need, and the range of other people that they think might be involved. We will see in Chapter 4 how a range of different data-collection methods can be used in an action research project, and what will become immediately obvious is that the cooperation of colleagues, pupils and others will be essential in terms of responding to questionnaires, agreeing to be interviewed or take part in focus groups, and so on. Prior to starting off, it is important to ensure that people will agree to support the project in these ways, and that the proposed time frames are suitable for them. It is also a good time to consider what data you might require access to. Bearing in mind that schools and other settings hold large quantities of data, much of it very sensitive, you will need to think carefully just what school-based information you will need, and arrange access to it – if possible. This qualifier 'if possible' is highly important, as, if it is not possible, then the project may be put at risk. In the planning stages, it is vital to find out just exactly what you will and will not have access to. While a refusal may seem inconvenient during the planning phase, if your first discovery of its unavailability is part way through an important project, the matter is likely to have much more serious consequences. A revision of a proposal is a much smaller-scale inconvenience than having to effectively abandon, or only part complete, a well-established project.

A different dilemma: what is the question?

Another dilemma can be that of not having an immediately obvious question. Typically articulated as 'I'm interested in something to do with learner autonomy/behaviour/attitudes towards mathematics', the proposer brings no further clarity to an initial meeting with a tutor. Unlike Lauren, a teacher-student in this position feels some trepidation prior to the meeting, feeling that they should know exactly what they want to do, and have some sort of initial plan. Paradoxically, this situation is one which tutors can feel more able to deal with, and can in fact mean less worry or tension for the proposing teacher than can be the case when a well thought out proposal is deemed unsuitable.

The 'something to do with' approach is one which lends itself to action research particularly well. Elliott's 1991 model articulates a 'general idea' as its starting point, and the initial, or reconnaissance phase of the project is designed to clarify that into more focused questions and action hypotheses through a process of initial data gathering.

Katya teaches in an early years unit, and has a particular interest in early language development. She is approaching the final stages of a master's programme, and is trying to formulate a focus for her final dissertation. As her first meeting with her university tutor approaches, she feels concerned that she still has not sharpened her focus. She confides in a colleague who completed a similar programme some years before.

Katya gets things clear

Kayta arranges to chat to her colleague over coffee. Feeling at a very low ebb, she confides that she may not be able to complete her MA, as an essential skill of this last section is the development of a viable research proposal. She knows what she is really interested in, but feels that it is much too messy to form a research proposal. Remembering earlier advice to keep her focus small scale and simple, she thinks that her interests in language and play are too large and 'untidy' to allow her to formulate a suitable proposal. She feels that she will not be able to clarify her ideas sufficiently to satisfy her tutor and tells her colleague that she is now going to withdraw from the remainder of the programme.

   Her colleague allows her to talk, recognising that sharing the worry is an important first step in helping her get back on course. She skilfully steers the conversation, allowing Katya to articulate the various aspects of her practice that both interest and concern her. Within 10 minutes, she has confirmed that Katya is interested in early language development, and also in children's play. Rather than telling her how she thinks that these areas of interest might be clarified, and even combined into a research proposal, she suggests that, since there is still a week before Katya is due to meet her tutor to discuss the proposal, she keep a diary in the meantime, and use it to jot down any incidents or events that seem potentially meaningful. She reminds Katya that a diary can be used in a variety of ways in an action research project, and that one of its important functions is to act as a 'think-space' as the project unfolds. Perhaps, she suggests, this might begin to happen even before the project actually starts. Katya, somewhat encouraged by the response of her colleague, but still unsure, agrees to try out this form of diary-keeping.

Commentary

Even when the practitioner has a broad area of interest, there may still be a difficulty in translating it into a well-focused research proposal. The complexity of educational practice means that any particular aspect of one's practice does not exist in isolation, and thus disaggregating a set of tangled issues into a more manageable format can initially seem almost impossible. Katya was clearly experiencing the effects of such complexity, and was unable to see a way through this. Her diary there-fore has no particular structure, but simply contains descriptions, thoughts, comments, reflections and questions about her experiences during the week. Altrichter et al. (2008) describe the research diary as

'A companion in the research process'. This simple statement is a powerful illustration of the extent to which a diary is useful in research. Like any companion, it provides support, guidance, clarification and, at times, challenge. If we use the analogy of the research project as a journey, then the diary-companion should also be central in the planning stages. Because the next chapter deals with the use of a diary as a data collection tool in action research, this commentary focuses on its use primarily as an initial clarificatory and planning device.

Reflecting on Katya's situation I was reminded also of my own feelings when completing my DPhil using an action research approach. The dynamic nature of action research meant that my focus could shift and, at times, I was left with a feeling of having lost focus completely. Comparing my own progress to that of a colleague who was completing archival research for a history PhD, I recorded in my diary: 'I seem to need loads of thinking time – and sometimes I don't even know what I'm thinking about. Is he better at his work than I am? He certainly seems to have a much clearer focus.' A later entry, however, reflecting the process of diary-keeping, indicated how useful I had found it as a place in which to make sense of things: 'The diary was at times my compass for that journey, and at other times, a resting point – I could use it to stop for a while, look round me, and at times, see a way forward.'

The reflective diary: a focusing device

Over the next week, Katya also began to see this potential in diary-keeping. The day before meeting her tutor, she takes time to reflect on what she has written, and quickly recognises some key themes emerging. One question she had noted at the end of a role-play session, which she hardly recalls writing, suddenly appears to be highly significant. As she ponders over it and reflects on her conversation with her colleague, she realises that using the diary in this way had allowed her to see that her interest in language development and play could in fact be clearly related in a simple but powerful way. Her jotted question in the diary 'how can I give them better role-play games?' helped her question just what she meant by 'better', and from that, see that what she was actually looking for, was to give the children role-play situations that were highly meaningful to them and, through this, give them opportunities to develop better language skills. She began to see that her difficulty in clarifying a focus was actually due to the fact that it involved both of her interests in a relational way. She was, in fact, able to articulate a rather straightforward focus in the 'I want to change . . . because . . .' format suggested by Baumfield et al. (2008: 15).

This format is one of a number of 'starting points for enquiry' listed by Baumfield et al. (2008: 15) which can help turn the more abstract initial area of interest into the more concrete research focus. Structures such as

- I would like to improve . . .
- I want to change . . . because . . .
- I am perplexed by . . .
- I think . . . would really make a difference to . . .
- I am particularly interested in . . .

provide 'hooks' on which researchers can hang their ideas.

When the search for clarification of an initial messy idea proves challenging, the use of questions like these can provide a useful testing device. Attempts to articulate the general idea in one of these (or other similar) formats, can both check the focus as suitable for an action research project, and also clarify it as a viable project.

Conclusion and summary

This chapter explores two key ways in which people undertaking action research projects may have difficulties in getting started on them. On the one hand, Lauren's efforts to draw up an action research proposal with an existing question in mind, illustrate the degree to which our own enculturation can make the process a real challenge. Although if asked to describe our practice, we use words like complexity, unpredictable, nuanced, evolving, personal, passion and so forth, when we consider researching that practice, we seem to default to a more positivistic mode. Whitehead (2006) in a seminar for his research students suggests that 'a living theory approach is easy to comprehend but difficult to embody in the cultural formations and power relations that influence what is recognised as valid knowledge in the Academy'. Suggesting that 'the ease of comprehension is that the approach resonates with what individuals know about the lives they live', he further articulates the ways in which power relations in schools and organisations can influence us to act in a way counter to our understanding and values and describes such 'living contradictions' and their identification and exploration as key elements in the start of an action research project.

The second study, that of Katya, paradoxically illustrates the way in which the complexity of practice is difficult to articulate as a valid and manageable research focus. The search for a simple articulation of the complex may seem counter-intuitive at first, but failure to achieve it means that many research projects never really fulfil their potential. Mertler (2009: 46–7) suggests that if the research topic lacks focus, is 'too vague', then 'the researcher may become overwhelmed with too many possible variations in the data collection, too much data, and too little time'.

Getting started on an action research project is thus a complex and time-consuming process, which may need support and guidance. It may take longer than anticipated, involving explorations of both philosophical and pragmatic matters. Those undertaking action research projects for the first time should take heart from the fact that even with experience, these challenges remain. My own research diary entry from the third year of DPhil study through action research, having already completed a three-year master's degree through action research, illustrates my own frustrations as I found myself continuously pulled back into the culture and language of school accountability: 'This action research hasn't really been my thing – every time I think I've got into that way of thinking, I get lost again.'

My hope is, that as you read this, you feel some comfort that the dilemmas you experience in your work, and will continue to experience, are ongoing dilemmas for most, if not all action researchers.

We finished this chapter with a case study illustrating the use of a diary in clarifying a project starting point. The more commonly known use of a research diary is that of a source of research data, and reflective/reflexive engagement with the project as it unfolds. The next chapter explores these notions further.

Further reading

Baumfield, V., Hall, E. and Wall, K. (2010) *Action Research in the Classroom*. London: Sage.

Koshy, V. (2010) *Action Research for Improving Educational Practice: A Step-by-step Guide*. London: Sage.

Mertler, C. (2009) *Action Research: Teachers as Researchers in the Classroom*. London: Sage.

Each of these books provides a structured overview of action research in an accessible and readable manner. While they differ in their emphases and structures, it may be useful as a new action researcher to dip into each. Personal choice is important in finding texts that support your own personal learning, while at the same time, the need to allow your reading to take you outside and beyond your normal practice is a key part of that learning.

Additional online resources can be found at:
www.sagepub.co.uk/beraseries.sp

CHAPTER 4

COLLECTING, COLLATING AND CONVERSING WITH DATA

This chapter explores data; its nature, collection, collation and meaning. Case studies and exemplars are used throughout the chapter to illustrate and explore the ways in which we identify appropriate data, plan and undertake its collection, collation and analysis. Through these discussions, we also address the practicalities, ethical issues, intellectual rigour and integrity of action research.

The importance of early data collection, the initial reconnaissance phase, is also emphasised in this chapter, as is the initial analysis process. Through this, we begin to develop an understanding of the concept of data-driven, theory-generative approaches in research.

What counts as data?

On starting an action research, or indeed any other research project, for many practitioners, this question is one of the first asked once a focus has been clarified, and forms a key part of the early planning process. It is important for me to clarify my use of terminology in respect of the word 'data'. While for some people this word has resonances of the type of 'hard data' produced through large-scale surveys or other quantitative means only, I use it to mean all those items of information gathered in the course of a research project. Further, I use the word 'evidence' in relation to the *use* of data. The argument built around a particular set of data is what constitutes the 'evidence' for any claims made by the research.

Deciding what counts as data, and then which data to collect, will help guide the planning of the project, negotiation of access to the field, and appropriate timescales to be drawn up. For the beginning action researcher, this question may not be as simple as it first appears. Chapter 2 introduced some models of the action research process and it is possibly at this stage of a project that closer conversation with these models becomes important. As an iterative process of review, reflect, observe and act, the data collection phase of an action research project is neither epistemologically nor temporally removed from the analysis or the action in the project. Indeed, for action research as a project which often has its genesis in a 'hunch', or a 'general idea', the very notion of 'data' within the project is not only potentially challenging at the start, but almost certainly changes conceptually and substantively during the life of the project. Given that action research is also a data-driven approach to research, the questions relating to data are vitally important in getting the project off to a good start.

Quantitative and qualitative

In order to effectively address these questions so that data collection, collation and analysis can be properly planned, it is imperative to return to the research question itself. The nature of the data required in any research project is highly dependent on the actual research question. This might seem a rather obvious, indeed superfluous, statement but experience of supervising countless projects has shown me that many inexperienced researchers come to their projects with fixed notions of how they will collect their data. First, cultural orientation to 'scientific' and 'objective' concepts cause many to view the process of data collection as leading to quantifiable, objective measures of the phenomena in question. Secondly, emerging understanding of social science methodologies suggests to many new researchers that most projects in this broad genre use questionnaire and interview as the predominant data collection devices. This is often coupled with an assumption that the qualitative data produced from a questionnaire will be converted to numeric form, and thus made more legitimate. Qualitative data such as interview transcripts may be seen as sources of less reliable evidence, and it is not unusual to see action research assignments for postgraduate programmes include summary tables of questionnaire responses in the text, which are then explained and analysed, while interview transcripts are found in the appendices, and barely referred to in the main text. In some way, the initial 'sense' of the research question can get lost at this stage, and the whole process turn into a more mechanistic one than it might be. It is also likely that the data presented will not have actually addressed the research question. Questions about children's enjoyment of their work may be answered with data showing improved test scores (which *may* be proxy measures, but cannot be assumed to be so). Qualitative data will often be identified as relevant, but is often dealt with in a quantification framework. The propensity to interpret a range of well-produced graphs and charts as the effective presentation of research findings is probably somewhere in most of us.

Further, and it is worth introducing a cautionary note here, 'qualitative' and 'quantitative' are sometimes used as descriptors of research approaches or methodologies (often thought of as almost polar opposites in their philosophies). I do not subscribe to that view, but instead consider these words to be descriptors of data types. As such, any research approach can make use of both types of data. Action research is no exception, and indeed a quantitative data set can provide a very useful backdrop to a study, illustrating perhaps a broader significance of your own research question. The more qualitative data can then be used to provide insight into the situation.

Let us start exploring the 'data' question in a little more detail by introducing the story of Judy, a pastoral leader in a secondary school, to illustrate the stages in her project, and the ways in which data were generated and dealt with.

Judy and the behaviour problems

Case study part 1

Judy was an experienced teacher working in a mixed-sex secondary school in an inner-city area. Indicators of deprivation were a little above the average, but not significantly so, and on the whole the school had a good reputation. The school had undergone a reorganisation in its pastoral structure, and single-sex, relatively small tutor groups operated in Key Stage 3. While this had initially caused some consternation among staff, now in its second year of operation it was felt that behaviour problems had subsided and those which persisted were more effectively managed. Early indications suggested that achievement was also improving. Judy had a tutor group of 15 year 8 boys who seemed to be the focus of every negative conversation in the classroom. During the autumn term, they had had more disciplinary and behaviour incidents logged than the rest of the year group in total. Their attendance was beginning to drop off also and, even in her own lessons with them (geography), they had begun to be troublesome. The typical pattern revolved around persistent, but often low-level disruption such as calling out, 'messing around' with other pupils, causing minor distractions and, at times, 'answering back'. The boys were of average ability, one was receiving support because of dyslexia, and one had mild attention deficit hyperactivity disorder (ADHD) for which he received some in-class support on a daily basis. All teachers in the school had attended INSET training in relation to general behaviour management, and in relation to specific needs, such as ADHD, children on the autistic spectrum and dyslexia.

At the start of her action research project Bernadette formulated her research question as follows:

'What can I do to help improve the behaviour of the boys in my tutor group?'

Commentary

Judy has clearly formulated a typical action research question and, following Elliott's model, decides that her starting point is to undertake a reconnaissance. Other authors describe this as scoping or mapping out the field. In the words of McNiff and Whitehead (2005) the researcher is asking 'What do I already know about the issue?' This is an important starting point, and indicates the need to consider all the possible sources of information about the matter in question. To reiterate the words of Popper, 'We must first get better acquainted with the problem.' (Popper, 1972: 260)

It is important to recognise and remember that the articulation of a hunch or perception needs further exploration before it can be translated into a legitimate research focus. A feeling on the part of a practitioner that something may not be quite right, or in some way problematic, is not necessarily grounded in 'fact'. It could arguably be the case that a practitioner such as Judy is feeling somewhat sensitive about her group's behaviour, and therefore her initial hunch is as much a manifestation of personal sensitivity or security as it is of any reality. To ameliorate this, and to justify her engagement on a research project, it is imperative that some further substantiating evidence is sought. In this case, Judy, in order to consolidate (or otherwise) her own perception of the problem, has also consulted school records such as behaviour logs and attendance records. Together with her own hunch, they convince her that there is an issue worth exploring. What the records do not do, however, is help her understand what the nature of that problem or issue is. They do not get her better acquainted with her problem.

When considering sources of data through which a practitioner might do this, it must be remembered that there may be many differing perspectives on an issue, and it is necessary to get a wide range of views in order to capture as full a picture as possible. This does not necessarily involve selecting a large number of respondents or participants. If they all represent a similar perspective, then your evidence could still be rather skewed. What is important is that you consider what those sources of information and data might be, and deliberately seek a wide range.

The action researcher is trying to delve into what is happening or what has happened and, as such, needs to ensure that this initial reconnaissance phase frames the rest of the project effectively and accurately, and is informed by as complete a range of perspectives as possible.

Reflection

Consider Judy's situation, and make a list of sub-questions she might ask in relation to her focus. Some starting points might be:

- What is the nature of the unacceptable behaviour?
- When and how often does it occur?
- Who is involved?
- Is there any pattern?

For each of these (and others you identify) compile a list of the sources and types of data that might help her get a better understanding of her problem. Remember that it is important for her to consider the problem from all angles. Consider also, for each source of data, the pragmatics of accessing and collecting them. Will Judy find it easy or difficult to access the data? Will she need any special permission? Ethical matters will be discussed in more detail later in the chapter, but at this stage, list and start to reflect on what you think the ethical issues might be in relation to each source.

Do you think there are any ethical issues apart from those associated with data?

Case study part 2

Judy spends some time reflecting on her initial question. Having attended many behaviour management training events in her 15 years' teaching, she has a range of resources at her fingertips and has become adept at using them. This time, however, her own initial pause for reflection makes her consider the appropriateness of using some 'off-the-shelf' behaviour management scheme. She decides to keep a reflective diary for a two-week period before deciding on anything further. Previous experiences in using approaches have been variously successful, but her reflections also make her realise that they have often been most effective when she has adapted them, or used some of their principles tailored to her own situation. She is initially unsure what exactly she should record in the diary, but decides that if she records quite widely at first, then perhaps the significance of her notes may emerge later. She begins therefore to note particular events, brief accounts of incidents in class, or reported to her, recording an account that is more than just an event log. She notes thoughts, reflections, questions and feelings relating to the events. Although she usually records all school-related events electronically, she feels that a dedicated notebook would allow her more scope in terms of keeping a reflective diary. She ensures that each entry is carefully dated (and with the time, if appropriate), and leaves plenty of space for later reflections, thoughts and questions as they may arise.

Commentary

Judy has begun to realise the importance of reflection in action research. Day (1993) considers reflection to be a necessary (though not sufficient) condition for professional learning and development, and in discussing its significance, identifies that it provokes 'confrontation' of that learning in a way that informs future action. The Ghaye and Ghaye (1998) model of reflection was introduced in Chapter 2. Other such models, such as those of Smyth (1991), Griffiths and Tann (1991) and Rolfe et al. (2001), provide a range of frameworks and approaches, and likewise provide an imperative to action. Later in the chapter we discuss the nature and structure of the reflective diary in more detail.

During the two-week diary-writing period Judy captures stories from practice, anecdotes from the classroom and staffroom, near-verbatim transcripts of pupil and colleague discussions, and a record of her own thoughts and feelings over the period. In short, she has begun to build up a story of what is happening, in a more systematic manner than she had previously done. She is beginning to gain an insight into the nature of the behaviour problem, the perspectives of pupils and colleagues, and her own response in relation to it. As yet, however, she is unsure whether or how it can be called 'data'. Reading over the entries for the past two weeks, like many new researchers, she finds that her questions are of the type, 'That's all very well, but is it data? Can it be used in my project? If so, how?'

It can be tempting to think that such anecdotal evidence is inadmissible in 'real' research. Vandenbroucke (2006), however, in his discussion of the strength of study designs in relation to their intended outcomes, identifies anecdotal case study and report as the most effective design in studies whose focus is discovery and explanation. Although writing in the field of medical studies, I would suggest that his analysis is germane in most contexts. Suggesting that 'odd observations . . . in data or the literature' will spark new ideas, he identifies this as the source of further analysis and discovery.

Thus, Judy's own diary of anecdotal evidence is indeed part of the legitimate data for her project. Not only will it help her in building the narrative of her project, but quotations from it can be used to illustrate her own perception of events as they were uncovered, her responses to them and her developing understanding of their importance. Alongside other key data sources, her diary will form part of a well-rounded evidence base for the project. It will also of course contain more than anecdotes, as is discussed in the next section of this chapter.

Having now listed some the sub-questions that Judy might ask, and the means by which she might gather relevant data, let us now further consider the range of data sources that may be useful to her and to action researchers in general. The list of possible sources can include, but is not restricted to:

- reflective diaries and critical incident approaches
- interviews
- questionnaires
- document analysis
- observations of practice.

The rest of this chapter provides an overview of data collection techniques, exploring their appropriateness in particular situations, and discussing pragmatic issues around them, and some possible ethical considerations.

Data sources

The intensely personal nature of an action research project, with its focus on reflective practice, is perhaps a key difference between it and other forms of practice-based research. For this reason, I intend to discuss the use of self-reflective means of data collection first, and in more detail than other data collection methods. Of primary importance in this set of methods is the reflective diary. I begin by discussing the diary, its use and approaches to its analysis, and also introduce the relationship between critical incident techniques and diary-keeping. While Judy has already begun keeping a diary, a more fully developed strategy for this is likely to be of benefit throughout the project. Throughout this section on data collection I draw on examples from my own research, using them to illustrate some of the key issues raised.

The reflective diary

The case study has drawn attention to Judy's use of a reflective diary in her research. Almost universally used in action research projects, it can form both the narrative and chronology of the project, as well as provide a thinking space. The format of this diary is entirely up to the researcher. What is important, is that the format is easily accessed and used, that the researcher feels comfortable with it, and that it is used on a regular basis.

For many action researchers, a key question at the start is 'What should I write in the diary?' As in many action research questions, there is no right answer. However, that is not to say that there are no guidelines. It is, of course, important that if the diary is to provide a chronology of events, it is completed (and dated) on a regular basis with descriptions of events, as they happen. It is a good habit to write something in the diary at least once each day, even if it is just something relatively short. These daily entries can also form prompts for reflection, both in the moment and later. In this way, they help develop understanding and analysis. Moon (2006: 26–36) suggests that:

- Journals slow the pace of learning
- Journals increase the sense of ownership of learning
- Journals acknowledge the role of emotion in learning
- Journals give learners an experience of dealing with ill-structured material
- Journals encourage metacognition (learning about one's own process of learning)
- Journals encourage learning through the process of writing.

Regular diary writing keeps the research question, and thoughts about it, continuously to the fore in the researcher's mind and, as such, provides the opportunity for personal, and indeed emotional engagement with the research topic and process. Saunders (2004) suggests that the evidence base in considering practice is a living process built around practical experience. Citing Dadds (1995), she describes the process as passionate enquiry. In the text 'Passionate enquiry and school development',

Dadds herself suggests that Vicki's enquiry (Vicki is a teacher whose story is related in the text) is informed as much by feelings as by thoughts. The diary can be a safe place in which to record those feelings.

The regular writing of a diary is significant also in its contribution to increasing what Mason (2002) calls 'sensitivity' within the research. Despite our familiarity with our own practice, the keeping of a diary and other self-reflection/self-study techniques almost always reveal something previously hidden to us. In short, the diary can be seen as a way of producing a running commentary on the project, to record observations and, crucially, a space in which to begin the process of theorising practice in order to develop contextualised understanding of specific problems or concerns.

The use of such techniques in conjunction with other sources of practice observation data (such as that from other adults, or pupils in the room) can provide a valuable means of *triangulation*, that is, comparing and contrasting different perspectives (either from different sources or different data collection tools) in order to find points of agreement, points of disagreement or areas of incomplete understanding or further interest; all possible pointers to the formulation of a new action research cycle.

Using diary data

While diary-keeping is fundamentally a private and personal business, the research diary will also contain elements that the writer may wish to make more public. The final report may include some citation from the content of the diary, but it is often the analysis of the diary that features most strongly in the report. I have chosen not to discuss at this point the way in which diary entries may be analysed, but rather keep it for later in the chapter, relating it also to other sources of unstructured, text-based data in the project, and at this stage focus on where it can be useful in the project.

Excerpts from the diary can, on occasion, feature in the final report. One example might be to show how thinking has changed over the course of the project. The example below is from my own diary entry during my DPhil study. Having spent some time wondering why so few girls were choosing to study A-level physics, and what I, as a classroom teacher, could do to make the subject more attractive, I was uncovering perspectives that really challenged my initial understanding. I had a reluctance at the time to simplify (as I thought it would be) my focus to one simply of feminism, and felt that to do so, would in fact be an 'easy' way through a much bigger philosophical problem. As I analysed interview data with a range of students I began to see a strong theme of the mathematicisation of physics coming through, and a student perception of both mathematics and physics as lacking in creativity, and defined by non-negotiable rules and a somewhat Boolean approach to logic. From my perspective, this was highly significant, and confirmed my own perception that it was not a simple 'girls don't like physics' matter. It was more than that. Couched in the epistemology of the subjects themselves, in their very nature, the analytic framework was one of philosophy in the wider sense. What did this evidence mean for me as a teacher? Did physics have to have this epistemology? Was this an essential part of its nature? Had it always been?

I then undertook what could be described as a *conversation* between my data and 'the literature', trying to understand this theme of rules and logic, and, through the history of science and science education, began to understand the provenance of the curriculum I was teaching at the time. My diary entry reflected the change in my understanding that followed my analysis and reading (and in fact, writing it in my diary was also the place where I 'worked it all out', or had conversations in my head), and raised questions about my own practice:

Example 1

I've been reading some contemporary literature on women in science. It seems that the whole thing about logic, and mathematical rules, and no creativity, *is* in fact a gender issue. I never thought of it that way. It seems that girls and boys deal with rules differently, and that the way physics presents them suits boys rather than girls! That seems peculiar to me; I'd never thought of it that way, but there does seem to be a lot of fairly recent research indicating that the way the content, and the methods of science are presented to students is biased in favour of boys. I wonder if that's the case? I suppose that's really two questions. Do boys and girls see logic and rules differently, and is science education really based on that type of model? What would I see if I examined my own classroom?

Using the diary entry in this form, almost as a 'pause for reflection' in the narrative of the project, not only identified the questions that had become important for the next phase of my action research, but gave some insight into the way in which they had arisen. It was, in essence, an auto-dialogic process, in which I began to make meaning from data, informed by wider consideration and reading.

While it is probably unusual for relatively large extracts from a diary to make their way into a report, especially a report which is fairly short in length, it is not at all uncommon to see action research reports draw on diaries to illustrate changes in thinking, near verbatim reports from practice (such as an exchange with a colleague or pupil), or an affective response to a particular situation. A further example from my DPhil diary illustrates this:

Example 2

My diary entry of late August 1999 indicates that 'talking things over' is still something I value very much in terms of helping me clarify my thinking and makes me think too about how little the children really get the chance to do this in their learning.

This realisation was in fact for me, what Tripp (1993) and others would call a *critical incident*, which he describes as things that mark 'significant turning points or changes in a person' (1993: 8). What, then, makes an incident 'critical'? While a number of writers have addressed this, they mainly draw on the early work of Tripp (1993) and Woods (1993), who both emphasise the extent to which their identification is based on the judgement of the researcher after the incident has occurred. In my experience, researchers have found this a very helpful construct in the analytic rereading of reflective diaries. The identification of critical incidents in their practice, or in their thinking, can be powerful stimuli for further research or action.

Tripp (1993: 8) suggests that critical incidents are not

> things which exist independently of an observer . . . awaiting discovery like gold nuggets or desert islands, but . . . are created. Incidents happen but critical incidents are produced by the way we look at a situation: a critical incident is an interpretation of the significance of an event. To take something as a critical incident is a value judgement we make, and the basis of the judgement is the significance we attach to the meaning of the incident.

Woods (1993: 357) suggests that critical incidents are 'unplanned, unanticipated and uncontrolled. They are flash-points that illuminate in an electrifying instant some key problematic aspect of the teacher's role and which contain, in the same instant, the solution'.

As such, and of necessity, a critical incident only becomes critical in retrospect. Their identification happens only on reflection. They are not classified as 'critical' due to any drama or sensationalism attached to them. Rather, their criticality is based on the justification, significance, or meaning given to them by participants (Angelides, 2001). A reflective diary can provide a rich seam of potentially critical incidents and their analysis can significantly inform the progress of an action research project.

I have found Tripp's guidelines for critical incident analysis supportive and epistemologically helpful. In short, these can be presented as follows:

1 Describe an incident from recent professional practice, choosing something interesting, annoying, inspiring, thought-provoking or typical.
2 Suggest an initial explanatory response to the incident (including your emotional response).
3 Ask questions which delve deeper into the meanings behind the incident, for example, different ways of thinking about it. Keep asking why; explore your dilemma, consider personal theories and values that influence your judgement.
4 Consider the implications of the incident and your deeper understanding of it on your future practice. (Adapted from Tripp, 1993)

This approach (and a simple template derived from it) has been of use to many action researchers trying to make sense of diary entries. For others, critical incident analysis becomes a deliberate choice of method in its own right. These researchers often choose to use a template, such as that in Figure 4.1, to help them capture and initially explore such incidents.

Reflection

Reflect on your own practice in recent weeks. Has anything happened which you now, in retrospect, might class as 'critical'? Use the template (based on Tripp's work) to record and reflect on your own development.

Interviews

Interviews often form the mainstay of the data for action research projects. Although time-consuming to carry out, they are particularly useful in helping the researcher to 'get inside' the story. On the whole, action research interviews tend to be of the 'semi-structured' variety. By this, I mean that the researcher will normally have some guideline questions around issues they want to explore, but will have flexibility in how the questions are worded, in how they lead to follow-up questions and in the order in which they are asked. The aim of the semi-structured interview is to allow both the researcher and the participant the freedom through which to explore an honest and authentic account. The more skilled the

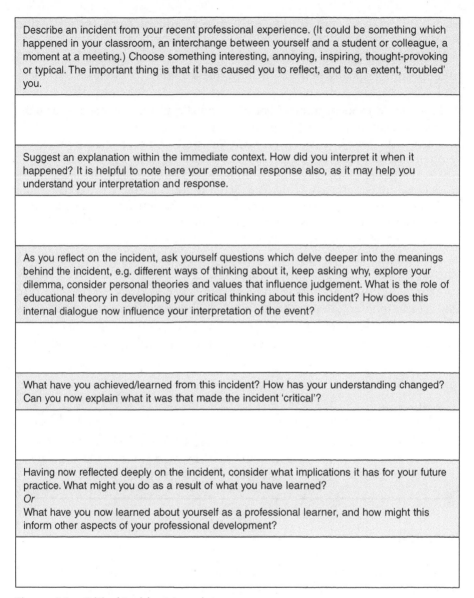

Figure 4.1   Critical Incident template

interviewer, the more the 'structure' can be relaxed, and the interview can become more of a conversation. However, it does take well developed skill on the part of the interviewer to ensure that such unstructured interviews remain focused on the main research question(s).

Becoming skilled in interview technique is usually as a result of experience. Early attempts at interviewing are often characterised by a more structured and somewhat formal approach. For this reason, I usually advise my own students/mentees to plan a period of time between the first and second interview they undertake so that they can reflect on and learn from the process itself. Regardless, however, of the skill and experience of the interviewer, there are some key points to consider in preparing to interview participants. Among those that are particularly pertinent to school-based researchers are:

- selection of interview participants
- location and time of the interview
- relationship between interviewer and interviewee
- ensuring encouragement during the interview without asking leading questions
- capturing the content of the interview.

These are in fact ethical considerations as well as pragmatic ones. Let us address each briefly in turn.

Selection of interview participants

Two things are of central importance in selecting participants for your interviews. First, a return to the initial research question is important, so that in remembering exactly what it is you want to find out, you begin to form a picture of who might be able to contribute useful information. For most educational researchers this will mean that interview participants can come from colleagues, pupils, those you manage or who manage you, and other professionals working in your setting. It is tempting to include groups such as parents or school governors in this list but, given the challenges you might face in undertaking such interviews, consideration should be given as to whether these voices are needed in relation to the research question. If your question relates to improving your own teaching of a particular subject or topic, then while the parent voice in relation to a pupil's natural interest in the subject might be of some interest, it is unlikely to provide you with the data that will allow you to effectively understand your own practice better and improve it within your context. However, if your question relates to motivating children to regularly complete homework tasks, then the parent voice will probably be essential to your study.

Secondly, it is necessary to remember that there will be a range of viewpoints and perspectives on any issue and, as a researcher, you must try to ensure that voices from all these perspectives, if possible, make their way into your data set. The process of 'triangulation' is explored in many texts, the key definitions indicating its role in ensuring validity of the data. Derived from the language of navigation, its main articulation is the comparison of data gathered by different methods and/or different sources. Thus, the researcher actively seeking out participants for interview who can provide differing perspectives is engaging in one aspect of the triangulation process. In this way the strength of claims made can be improved and, at the same time, points of disagreement flagged as areas of incomplete understanding; hence the development of continued exploration.

Throughout the selection process, however, pragmatic issues must be remembered. It may be that one particular person could bring a very important perspective into the research but, on asking them, they decline to take part. This is a very real issue, and sometimes a risk, in designing a project of this nature, and must be thought through carefully at the planning stage. If, for example, a person thought to have a vital voice declines to participate in the research, is it possible to get that perspective from an alternative source? If not, will its absence compromise the quality, or even the viability, of the research?

For this reason, the practical matters around planning a range of respondents, and gaining their consent to be interviewed, is vital early in the process. If key personnel do not wish to participate, then it is much better to know this at an early stage.

Location and time of the interview

It is to be expected the researcher is deeply interested in the project. It is not necessarily the case that others will share this passion. When participants agree to take part in a research project they are giving freely of their time as well as making a contribution to the project itself. Care should be taken in planning a location that will both show appreciation of this and set an atmosphere that will put respondents at ease. Privacy, protection against interruption and the comfort of both parties will all contribute to a more productive interview. The relationship between the interviewer and interviewee is also important in choosing an appropriate location. The use of his classroom, by a teacher to interview a pupil may highlight a power imbalance and make the pupil feel uncomfortable. Likewise, a senior leader interviewing a junior member of staff would be better choosing a neutral venue rather than their own office. Power relationships are an important and ethical consideration in any research, and perhaps even more so in action research which claims to be a democratic and democratising process.

Relationship between interviewer and interviewee

In action research, where the research is situated within the researcher's own practice, there will inevitably be issues of power relationships between the interviewer and interviewee. These may emanate from teacher–pupil or staff hierarchy situations, and must be taken into account in the conduct of an interview.

The teacher–pupil issue is also potentially problematic for school-based researchers. Inevitably, it raises questions of whether or not the pupil has actually felt they can refuse to participate, and what effect their participation may have on their life within the school. Will they feel able to respond truthfully? Will they find it hard to understand the nature and purpose of the research? Will they feel uncomfortable when asked probing questions?

There are issues, of course, for the teacher also. Will they be able to help the pupil feel comfortable and unthreatened? Will the pupil tell 'the truth' and produce useful data? In some ways, these issues can be addressed though careful planning of the location for the interview. Conducting it at a teacher's desk, with the teacher at one side and the pupil at the other, is unlikely to facilitate frank and open dialogue during the interview. Likewise, choosing a location in the school that may have negative associations for pupils may not be wise either. If it is possible to use a room that is comfortable, not associated with normal teaching or disciplinary functions, and unlikely to be interrupted, then the quality of the interview may be improved.

While these examples seem specific to teachers and pupils, it is not difficult to extrapolate from them to other situations where there may be a power imbalance, and it is the responsibility of the researcher to consider this at the planning stage, and take any steps possible in order to mitigate the issues that may arise.

Ensuring encouragement during the interview without asking leading questions

For the novice researcher, this can be a particular challenge. Nervousness can make the interviewer stick rigidly to a script, with the effect that he or she may ask little in the way of follow-up, or probing questions. Doing this can reduce the interview to something more like an oral questionnaire, losing the rich data that it has the potential to generate. On the other hand, it is possible that the interjection of probing questions, if not managed carefully, can serve to move the interview in a particular direction, betraying the researcher's own interpretation or agenda, and in this way skew the information. Hasty interjections can exacerbate this and one technique that may be helpful is to seek clarification through rephrasing what has been said, thus confirming what is meant but also gaining some thinking time in which to develop a more considered probing question. 'So can I just confirm that what you mean is . . .?' helps both in reducing the potential for misinterpretation, and also the rushed move to the next stage in the interview.

Capturing the content of the interview

Interviews have the potential to produce large quantities of unstructured, free-text data and, as such, a key decision accompanying the decision to undertake interviews is that of how to capture and record the interview. The options available include note-taking during the interview, writing up immediately after the interview and audio-recording during the interview. My own preference in this matter, and indeed my practice, is to audio-record if at all possible. This must be done with the permission of the interviewee, but in my experience it is unusual for participants to refuse. After an initial feeling of self-consciousness, they generally stop noticing a small recording device. Audio-recording obviates the need to focus on the recording process, and allows the interviewer to interact more thoughtfully with the interviewee content. In this way, both the interviewer and interviewee can feel more relaxed, the interviewer can listen more sensitively to the responses, and the interviewee can feel that the flow of what they are saying is not constantly broken by the interviewer pausing periodically to take notes.

However, this obvious benefit also has the potential to generate more text than might have been the case, and so the problem of how to later deal with the audio-recording is one to consider. Should the interviewer make notes from the recording? Should a full transcript be produced? Should the services of a transcriber be used? Many texts deal with the pros and cons of each, and of course the decision made is often one of pragmatism rather than philosophy. What is important is that we return to the notion of action research as a data-driven, theory-generative methodology, recognising that it is perhaps more important to consider how you, as a researcher, might get to know this data in the best way possible. If you are fortunate enough to have the services of someone to transcribe interviews for you, then it is imperative that time is taken to read, reread and otherwise become immersed in the data.

As a final word on this matter, it must be remembered that the write-ups from the interview (whether in note form or as full transcriptions), like all data, remain the property of the respondent/participant, and should therefore be agreed as an accurate record or data set, and also, agreed in relation to their final use.

Questionnaires

If there is a need for data that can be quantified, for example, in response to a question about how widespread a particular perception is, or the extent to which colleagues have used a particular resource in a range of situations, then a potent and cost-effective way is through the use of questionnaires. This is particularly the case in school-based research as questionnaires can be administered and collected with little effort on the part of the researcher. There is no requirement for participants to post the return document and, in general, response rates are high. For reasons such as these, many practitioner-researchers use questionnaires as a main source of data collection.

The design of the questionnaire may, however, be more time-consuming than initially considered. Common problems that all researchers can run into include:

- lack of clarity in their own mind in relation to what they hope the questionnaire will elicit
- ambiguity in the wording of the questions
- lack of planning in terms of how the data will be collated and analysed
- bias in the framing of the questions
- unreasonable expectations in relation to what can be learned from the responses
- a presentation and layout of the document that may not be user-friendly
- response categories which fail to meet the responses people want or need to make.

The use of non-specific language is an important consideration in writing a question. It is highly likely, for example, that the use of words such as 'regularly', will be open to a range of differing interpretations and therefore answers to questions along the lines of 'do you regularly undertake extra study in your own time?' with the option of a 'yes' or 'no' answer will generate relatively meaningless data. It is much better to give specific measured intervals in cases like these, so that the question might be reformulated as follows:

> Do you undertake extra study in your own time:
>
> a. Once a month or less often
> b. 2–4 times per month
> c. At least once a week
> d. More than 4 times per week

Reflection

Do you think this question would now tell a teacher all she or he wanted to know about a student's study habits? Do you think a further question might help? What would you ask?

Some problems of lack of clarity can be addressed through piloting the questionnaire before it goes live. Getting a number of people (of a similar demographic to the intended recipients) to answer it, and even provide feedback, can seem time-consuming, but in the long run, is time well spent. If, in a set of 10 questions, three are unclear to most of the pilot group, then it makes sense to either discount or change those questions.

The layout and presentation of the questionnaire is an important and often overlooked consideration. Endless pages of poorly laid out questions are unlikely to look inviting to potential participants. Likewise, an abundance of free-response questions make the process look like hard work.

Having decided on a set of questions, and determined that some free-response questions are vital to the quality of the information possible, the matter of how much space to leave for those free-response questions that you consider necessary is also important. The issue of free-response versus coded response questions is one which you also need to consider in relation to the validity of the questionnaire. On the positive side, using pre-coded responses sets up an effective system for data collation and thus aids analysis. On the other hand, if your pre-selected responses are not appropriate for the needs of the participants, then the approximations they use in making their selected response may not give an accurate data set. This can be further complicated if responses to open-ended questions seem inconsistent with those gained from the coded responses.

As a researcher, these questions need to be carefully considered at the start of the project, and for those undertaking school-based action research, a further layer of complication is added.

In many large-scale surveys, the data collection document will ask for some biographical/demographical information in order that appropriate generalisations can be made from the findings. Names are not normally asked for, as there will be no need to consider the relevance of individual responses. In the small-scale action research projects undertaken by most education practitioners, no such generalisations will be made. Further, in many cases, the questionnaire may be a precursor to follow-up interviews and, as such, there needs to be some identification on the questionnaire. This raises many issues for the action researcher. Will participants be as willing to participate if they are asked to put their name on the form? Will those who do participate answer as truthfully as they might have done on an anonymous document? How can confidentiality be assured? Again, and particularly important in educational workplaces, there are issues of power relationships and ethics. Again also, there are no right answers. There is, however, a need for the researcher not only to consider these issues, but to formulate a justified and justifiable response to them. What will you, as an action researcher, do in order to deal with these concerns?

Document analysis

In any practice-based research project there are likely to be documents available which will give both historical and contextual information to the researcher. These documents are of two broad types. In the first case, there will be a range of documents produced externally to the setting, such as legislative and policy documents (which can illustrate not only guidance for practice, but also some of the reasons behind its articulation), national and regional achievement and other data, against which schools and settings are often benchmarked. Documents produced within the setting, such as school or setting-based policies, minutes of meetings, schemes of work, reports of inspections and so forth, can all provide a history of the current situation and, as such, help provide a rationale and historical narrative for the chosen research project.

Observations (of practice)

In certain settings, the use of interview, questionnaire and other data collection approaches may be difficult to implement effectively. With small children, for example, the lack of reading, writing and oral communication skills may be suggestive of a more observational approach to data capture. Approaches to this range from the very structured Flanders Interaction Analysis Categories (FIAC) (1970) to the more unstructured naturalistic approaches described by Miles and Huberman where the researcher tries to acquire an 'empathetic understanding' of the situation as perceived by 'local actors' as if 'from the inside' (Miles and Huberman, 1994: 6).

As with all decisions of method, the purpose of the data collection should inform the choice. If, for example, a teacher is interested in reviewing the nature and quantity of classroom talk, then the FIAC structure will be a focused and highly appropriate tool. A tool like this can also be adapted for observations of other types of interactions, as can be seen in the exploration of interaction and communication between adults and children on the autistic spectrum undertaken by McAteer and Wilkinson (2009), where Melanie, a teacher in the school, had developed her own specific adaption of the FIAC schedule to suit the needs of her own project which had involved developing a customised adult–child interaction training approach. Knowing that she needed to conduct highly structured observations of the training sessions, she adapted the FIAC schedule to take account of the specifics of her situation. (It is worth reading her account to see her reflections on using this approach.)

If, on the other hand, the observation is more to see 'in general' what interactions, conversations and behaviours are happening, then a more unstructured and naturalistic approach will be the most appropriate. While this approach helps to overcome what McKernan (1997: 115) describes as the 'problems with interaction analysis categories', indicating that they 'do not take sufficient account of the substantive content of the behavior or message', it is an approach which has the potential to yield large quantities of disparate data. As Punch (1998) explains, undertaking observations of this nature necessitates a lengthy familiarisation with the data, and a willingness and ability to develop conceptual categories in a more grounded approach. There is also a very practical question for the researcher choosing this. How will they actually capture and record the observations? Will they write notes as they observe? Will they ask someone else to? (in the knowledge that someone else may not be as attuned to the subtleties of the situation as might be hoped, and additionally, will add a further interpretation layer to the data).

Whichever approach to observation is used, my advice is to video-record the observed session, and conduct the observation afterwards. The challenge of accurately recording observations in-the-minute is demanding, and risks oversights which may be significant. Further, in recording and re-watching the session, the researcher develops a greater familiarisation with the data, which is in itself an initial analytic device.

Other data collection methods

While the diary, interview and questionnaire often form the mainstay of many action research projects, they are by no means the only methods. The challenges of working with very young children, or those for whom communication or understanding may be a problem, may make interviews and questionnaires inappropriate. Further, the research question itself may suggest a type of knowledge or information that these methods cannot adequately provide. For this reason, the following techniques may also form part of the action researcher's armoury:

- focus groups
- photographs
- children's work/drawings.

The list is not exhaustive. Dadds and Hart (2001) use the term 'methodological inventiveness' to describe the ways in which action researchers may approach their endeavours. I will not explore each in detail as, on the whole, they draw on similar recording and analytic techniques as those methods already dealt with.

The use of photographs in research of any type is both potent and potentially problematic. While it is a technique often used in community and participatory action research projects where it can provide a means to both document and analyse lives and experiences, schools and other educational settings are often cautious about allowing its use. For this reason, and because it is a major discussion in its own right, I will do no more here than flag up its potential, but caution about its 'unapproved' use in schools and settings.

The use of children's drawings, again potent, but less problematic, will feature in relation to data analysis in the next section.

Analysis and presentation of data

If there is one underlying theme throughout this section, it is that of familiarity with the data. It can probably be best expressed as a set of questions. How familiar are you with your data? Are you steeped in it? Immersed in it? Quite simply, the better you know the data, the better the analysis.

In the first part of this section I focus more on the processes of dealing with free-text and unstructured data than on dealing with more structured data, often produced as a result of closed-response questions on questionnaires.

Because the design of closed responses is in itself an analytic device, it is normal practice to use the response categories as a means for collating and presenting the data collected. The use of tables or various diagrammatic or graphical presentations can be used to make the data accessible to the reader, and also to aid initial analysis. On a cautionary note, however, the facility on even the most basic software packages to produce a range of output types is often a temptation to approach the presentation question as one of technical Information and Communication Technology (ICT) use, rather than one of meaning-making and communication. Knowing your own data so well can make it hard to assess whether or not your chosen presentation is best for the 'cold' reader. Getting some honest feedback from a critical friend is always of benefit here. It is crucial that underpinning every analysis and presentation decision is the question, 'What does it mean and how can I communicate it effectively?'

Analysing unstructured or free text data

Given the unstructured and discursive nature of a diary (or other free-response/unstructured data such as that produced by naturalistic observation or unstructured interview), it is vital to consider carefully just how its contents can be analysed. Options for analysing such data include discourse analysis, conversation analysis (both of which deal in different ways with language and its construction) and thematic analysis (which looks for patterns of meaning). Of these, thematic analysis is both more accessible to practitioner-researchers in that it is not dependent on specialised theory, and is more relevant in that the purpose of the research is usually to uncover meaning. I briefly now address the way in which such thematic analysis can be undertaken and signpost the appropriateness of this process in the analysis of interview and other free-response data (such as from free-response questions on a questionnaire).

Of primary importance in the analysis is immersion in the data. Being familiar with the contents of the diary (or interview or open-ended question response in questionnaires) is of crucial importance in helping identify units of meaning within it. On a practical level, it is useful if the data can be collated in a way that gives space for annotation, identification of areas of interest, colour-coding or cross-referencing. Having the notes in electronic format helps significantly with this, and while some people opt to use software programs, in my experience, they are more helpful for larger-scale projects and the time and effort spent in learning them and setting them up for the project may be better spent getting started on the task manually. It is helpful to undertake this annotation process at least twice, using the combing of data in this way to produce the key themes that will inform the analysis.

Having completed this annotation, units of commonality or units of meaning should start to become evident. From these, broader categories can be formed and, hence, themes for analysis. These stages are iterative in nature, and subsequent attempts may yield different outputs to previous attempts. It is not unusual for researchers to underestimate the amount of time needed for such an exercise, bearing in mind that it may take a number of iterations before some degree of consistency is reached. The use of a critical friend or research partner can be helpful here and aid clarity of thought, providing a useful cross-check on possible interpretations. Likewise, cross-checking emerging meanings with other participants can aid both the reliability and the validity of the interpretation. Finally, having decided on the themes, pieces of evidence can then be assigned to each theme so that the end-product is in the form of a thematic 'picture' of practice.

This inductive process results in what is known as a theory-generative (as opposed to a theory-testing) analysis. Action research is often described as a *theorising* methodology in that it does not seek to test practice against externally generated theories, which often results in the exposition of what Carr (1980) described as 'a gap between theory and practice'. These gaps, he suggests, are endemic to the 'view that educational theory can be produced from within theoretical and practical contexts different from the theoretical and practical context within which it is supposed to apply'

(Carr, 1980: 65). The use of a theorising methodology should produce a theory of practice which is congruent with that practice.

Analysing non-text data

Data produced from non-text sources such as images and drawings may also need to be analysed. In many ways, the process is similar to that for text-based data. I will illustrate this with an example, again from my own DPhil study.

Example 3

Having become aware of the masculine epistemology of mathematics and physics I wanted to further explore just what *image* pupils had of scientists. Given that most of their experience of having been taught science was with women teachers (they were year 9 pupils in secondary school), I opted to use the simple Draw A Scientist Test (DAST) (see Mason et al. 1991), in order to see just what their perceptions of scientists were. I analysed the drawings produced according to the following categories drawn up by Chambers (1983):

- male
- white
- laboratory coat
- eyeglasses
- facial hair
- symbols of research
- symbols of knowledge
- products of technology
- captions.

I interpreted facial hair as any kind of hairstyle which could be thought of as abnormal (generally wild, unruly and spilling over the face). Symbols of research were interpreted as items of standard laboratory equipment, for example test tubes, Bunsen burners, bottles, batteries, etc. Symbols of knowledge were interpreted as phrases, comments, or equations designating knowledge or discovery, while products of technology are interpreted as computers or electronic sensing, control or logging devices.

Table 4.1 summarises the responses of these year 9 students to the DAST.

Table 4.1   Year 9 Draw a Scientist Test

Characteristic	Frequency	% occurrence
Male	19	90.48
White	21	100.00
Laboratory coat	9	42.86
Spectacles	13	61.9
Facial hair	15	71.43
Symbols of research	9	42.86
Symbols of knowledge	2	9.52
Products of technology	0	0.00
Captions	12	57.14

From the DAST exercise, it was evident that these students perceived scientists as white, spectacle-wearing males with strange or eccentric hairstyles. The use of an existing codifying system (Chambers, 1983) was helpful to me in this case, but it would have been possible also to derive these categories from the data themselves, in a manner similar to that outlined above. Presenting the data in tabular form was, I felt, a simple way to help me and my readers make meaning. A particular strength in using this data collection method, however, was that it gave the pupils freedom to draw what they might have found difficult to express (particularly to a science teacher), allowed the collection of a large data set in a relatively time-efficient way, and produced something that I felt was more powerful than if I had extracted some of these descriptors from interviews or focus groups with them. From my perspective, the image each child produced was a very powerful articulation of the fact that science was seen as somehow 'outside' their field of normality. Further, on discussing this later with the children, I realised, with some surprise, that many of the children viewed their science teachers more as members of the set 'teachers' than the set 'scientists'. A science teacher was considered much more similar to a music or geography teacher than to a scientist. The method therefore produced data that provoked further questions, a key feature of a theorising, data-driven methodology.

Ethics in action research

This is a complex matter and one which I hope to raise as a matter for ongoing contextualised reflection, rather than as something which is 'dealt with' in this chapter. It is perhaps more important to raise awareness of the nature of ethical issues in research, to develop a questioning approach to ethics, than it is to produce a set of 'ethical guidelines'. Too often dealt with as a set of procedures for 'permission' and 'anonymity', the matter can be reduced to both a simplistic and, more importantly, an unethical one. There are various sets of ethical guidelines available for researchers and, depending on the context of your research, there may be an in-house policy for ethical approval. Whichever guidelines you consult, it is important to treat them as a set of prompts for question and reflection, rather than a tick-list, often explained as 'I ensured that my research followed the ethical guidelines as outlined by "Key-Text"'. When reading someone's report of their research, I, like many of my colleagues, find this troubling. It tells me nothing specific about the problems they faced in their research, nor the ways in which they made decisions about those problems. Indeed, it seems to imply that, in having read such guidelines, researchers get 'right answers' to matters of ethics, and thus conduct ethical research. Thomas (2009: 147) sums up the highly complex nature of ethical decision-making as follows, 'ethical principles encompass some decisions and dilemmas that pit not just right against wrong, but balance one right action against another right action, taking into account the possibly conflicting interests of the parties involved. What is right for me, may not be right for you'. The ethical researcher must be aware of this complexity and able to make a decision that is predicated on an exploration of these matters, both justifiable and justified.

For many education practitioners the BERA's *Ethical Guidelines for Educational Research* (2011) is a key guide. Framed as an ethic of respect for

- the person
- knowledge
- democratic values
- the quality of academic research
- academic freedom

it explores and unpicks the meaning and significance of each of these within a range of different research contexts. If we reflect on one of these briefly in the context of a piece of small-scale practitioner research, then we can see how a more problematising approach to ethical frameworks can be used.

Reflection

Returning to the case of a teacher opting to interview a pupil as part of a classroom-based action research study, and considering the power relationships that exist, what steps do you think can be taken to clearly *show* that the teacher has operated within a framework of respect for the person?

(How) Do you think she can also ensure that she herself can be respected during the process?

Consider the ways in which the information from the interview will be used. In what ways might that inform her decision about 'respect for the person'? Can you see any compromises or choices she might have to make? How might she justify such compromises?

Summary

This chapter attempts to bring together some key issues around the business of 'dealing with data', taking us from a starting point of the nature of data, through to questions of analysis, presentation, quality and ethics. Hopefully, having read this, you will have begun to be aware that while there are many guidelines around the decisions you make in a research project, the blind following of guidelines is not in itself sufficient to ensure 'good research'. Indeed, underpinning all action research is a question of 'ought', rather than 'can', putting the onus on the researcher to consider not simply the operation of guidelines or procedures, but also their significance in moral and ethical terms.

Further reading

Burton, D. and Bartlett, S. (2009) *Key Issues for Education Researchers*. London: Sage.
Thomas, G. (2009) *How to do your research project*. London: Sage.

These two books come to mind immediately as having strong and well-focused chapters on data collection methods. While not written specifically as action research texts, like many general education research methods books they provide very useful chapters on matters of data and their analysis.

Prosser, J. (ed.) (1995) *Image-based Research: A Sourcebook for Qualitative Researchers*. London: Falmer Press.

If the bulk of your research data is based on images or photographs, then a text such as this may be useful for you. While it does not have an action research focus, nor even an education focus, it will be helpful in exploring options in relation to this type of data.

 Additional online resources can be found at:
www.sagepub.co.uk/beraseries.sp

CHAPTER 5

DEALING WITH THE LITERATURE

This chapter is written in memory of a dear friend, colleague and mentor, Kath Green (1946–2007)

The place and role of the literature in action research is frequently a matter for debate and discussion, and occasionally a contentious matter. For proponents of a purist grounded theory approach, the literature should follow the initial data collection and analysis, its choice being guided by the preliminary analysis. The function of the literature in this case is to help interrogate and illuminate the data, aiding analysis. Other action researchers, however, tend to a more traditional approach in the use of literature, using it as in most other research approaches, where one of the first tasks is to conduct the literature review. The function of this review is to explore and scope out the field, clarify the research approach, and provide a theoretic and analytic framework prior to data collection. This chapter explores and discusses each of these approaches and their place in action research.

What do we mean by the literature?

I want to first of all consider the way in which we understand the word literature in the context of a research study. Thomas (2009: 30) describes it as 'anything that represents the results of research or scholarship on a subject', while Johnson (2009: 75) refers to the literature review as 'an examination of journal articles . . . books and other sources related to your action research project'. Burton and Bartlett (2009) identify four key functions of the literature review, indicating that it should:

1 provide background information on the general area of study
2 describe and evaluate the context of the research (social, political, economic, educational, environmental, and so on)
3 consider and comment on what has already been written within the general area of investigation, looking particularly at the relationships (differences and similarities) between studies
4 discuss the relevance of existing research to the research focus and methodology (including any impact on the intended research outcomes).

The nature and definition of 'the literature' is also implicit in the advice given to researchers in relation to structuring and writing up their study. For those undertaking their action research study as part of a postgraduate qualification, they will very often receive the standard advice concerning the structure and presentation of a final dissertation. In short, the dissertation is normally described as some variation of the following chapter structure (which is based on one I have used with students undertaking a more theory-testing than theory-building approach):

1 Introduction and focus of study (including contextualisation and rationale for the study)
2 Literature review
3 Research question, design and methods/methodology
4 Data presentation and analysis
5 Data interpretation and discussion
6 Conclusions (and recommendations).

Bold (2012: 166–8) outlines a similar structure which had previously been used with students she had supervised. The chronology of these chapters positions, and hence defines, the literature review as something that is part of the preparations for the field work. Its role is to systematically map out the field, identifying what is known, not known, or controversial. In doing so, it can help clarify the research question, and provide the theoretical framework in which it is to be tested. Thus, our primary definition of 'the literature' tends to relate to the *substantive literature*.

There are, of course, other varieties of 'literature' that will and should inform an action research project. The project is normally undertaken from a position of also knowing some of the *methodological literature*.

Almost any award-bearing professional development course that requires some practice-research will require the reading of at least an introductory overview text to research methods/approaches. The decision to engage with a particular methodological approach, such as action research, will also suggest additional, more specific texts.

A third body of literature that is rarely discussed in relation to literature reviews, or use of literature, is the broad, diverse, unusually unplanned and serendipitously discovered literature that causes a moment of insight or illumination. Its significance (like the criticality of a critical incident), is only understood after it has been read. As Green (1999: 112) reflected, 'My central argument is that the justifications for my choice of literature can only come *after* the literature has been read and has made its contribution to the development of my thinking'.

Thus, to the substantive and methodological bodies of literature, I add a third; the *eclectic* literature. I now discuss each in turn, illustrating, where appropriate, with case studies.

Substantive literature

This is the literature relating to the subject matter of the study, and can be located by using appropriate key-word searches on electronic catalogues and databases. I am dealing with this first, as it is the first meaning that people normally ascribe to the term 'the literature'. The researcher will usually have some familiarity with it in the first instance, and then develop their knowledge in a more thorough and systematic way as the project develops. Thus, if a college leader is exploring ways in which educational change may be managed more effectively, the substantive literature will relate to theories of change, theories of leadership, issues of communication, interpersonal skills and so forth. The review of this body of literature might suggest that there are four key factors in the effective management of curriculum change. The leader can then frame their own study around these factors, designing and developing questionnaire items, interview questions and other data collection tools to gather information in relation to each of them. In this way, the literature review can act as both a planning device and a subsequent analytic device. Relating findings back to the initial literature, to confirm or disconfirm theories or theses, the whole project becomes one of testing local findings against more global ones.

There is some discussion as to whether or not this is how action researchers (should) engage with the literature in their project. From some perspectives, this is still an essential part of undertaking small-scale action research projects, as it provides the researcher with a solid knowledge of theoretical frameworks relating to the focus of their study. While they may not use this review in such a rigid planning way, it will guide and shape their study design, execution and analysis.

Other perspectives suggest that, like the exploratory case study, or perhaps ethnographic or narrative approaches, action research is theory-generative, rather than theory-testing. It is for this reason that many action researchers avoid consulting a body of substantive literature at the start of their project. Coming to their work without a preset theoretic framework, they hope that in this way, they can effectively read the data in a more naive way. Their approach mimics that of grounded theorists, requiring no preliminary literature review and the minimisation of preconceptions. While some commentators identify the *tabula rasa* as a prerequisite, in reality, this is unlikely, and the researcher will bring previous experiences and their associated theoretical perspectives to the project. However, dispensing with the initial review of substantive literature can allow them to reduce any further theoretical influence, and so conduct the research in a theory-discovery mode. In other words, they approach the process with an open, rather than an empty, mind.

My own personal preference is that the substantive literature follows the data, is chosen on its basis, guided by it, illuminating and interrogating it. In small-scale studies, I have found it to produce a more meaningful outcome in that being data driven, it is completely contextualised. It also prevents the researcher taking a wrong turn. In the case of Rhodes's study, described by Cain (2011) and discussed in Chapter 3 of this text, Cain identifies how Rhodes arrives at a questionable outcome, suggesting that, in interpreting her data she may have given 'more weight to her reading of the literature than to her empirical findings' (2011: 5). As a new researcher, the authority of the literature is compelling, and it can be difficult to have the confidence to produce non-confirmatory findings.

Peter's story, presented below, illustrates some of the ways in which this initial engagement with the literature is both alluring, and also potentially misleading.

Peter's story, part 1

Peter is a newly appointed member of a senior leadership team in his school which caters for children with mild and moderate learning difficulties. His particular concern at present is that he is trying to lead a small team of teachers in developing more effective links with parents. His working group was formed on the basis of concerns among some staff that parents could more effectively support their children's needs if they were more involved in working with school staff. Peter has never formally led a project of this type before, and is anxious to use the opportunity in two ways. First, he actually wants to make a difference in terms of working with parents, but he also, and possibly more importantly, wants to learn more about himself as a leader, and use the opportunity to help him develop his practice in that respect.

He starts his project by formulating the question 'How can I reflect on my practice as a leader in order to improve that practice?' Clearly, this is an action research articulation and, as such, he decides that he needs to use a range of data sources which will give him some information about his leadership style. He keeps a reflective diary for a period of four weeks, noting events as they happen, reflections on them, and occasional near verbatim comments from his team. He decides to formulate a questionnaire about his leadership style, distribute it to his team and, on the basis of the responses, conduct a further set of follow-up interviews through which he can more fully explore some of the points raised. He has been surprised that the team members have so readily agreed to this, but feels that the fact other members of staff have undertaken action research projects in school has probably helped everyone feel more at ease with discussing and sharing practice than they might otherwise have been. He is conscious, however, of some of the potential issues involved in interviewing the team. As a newly promoted member of staff, he realises that issues of power and position must be sensitively handled. Likewise, in a small school, while anonymity may be difficult, he must carefully preserve confidentiality.

He designs a short questionnaire, administers it to staff and, while he is awaiting its return, decides that he should do some reading around the subject of leadership. In doing so, he begins to realise that 'communication' in leadership seems a much more complex issue than he had thought. Reflecting on the last two meetings with staff, he decides that his own communication has been less effective than it might have been, and that this is something he must work to improve.

He immediately reflects on the ways in which he communicates with the team, and other members of staff in the school. On the basis of this, and his reading of the literature, he decides that his use of email is not effective. Prior to reflecting on this he had used it to remind team members about the weekly meetings and to distribute the agenda. He now decides that a personal communication to team members about scheduled meetings would be more effective, and so each week for the next three, he visits each member of the team the day before the meeting and gives them a paper copy of the agenda.

Commentary

Like many novice action researchers, Peter is anxious to do some reading so that he feels properly engaged in an academic research project. Although he has already started a process of data collection, and has another stage planned, he is influenced by what he has read, and decides that it provides him with a possible improvement strategy. The desire to read the literature too early, coupled with a desire to move to action can lead many novice (or indeed experienced) action researchers along a wrong path. His implementation of an action step is premature, and lacks the support of a well-analysed database. Green (1999: 106) describes the potential in a situation like this to 'give the study a false kind of clarity in its early stages'.

Reflection

If you were Peter's tutor or mentor, how might you advise him at this stage of his project? How do you think he might reach a more secure kind of clarity?

Peter's story, part 2

On the fourth week of Peter's visit to colleagues with the agenda for the team meeting, one of them asks if he will send it electronically also, adding that she much preferred it that way, she was less likely to lose it before the meeting, and she liked to be able to annotate it electronically and bring her tablet computer to the meeting. Doing this allowed her to refer back to her annotations and continue to take notes during the meeting, if necessary. Peter is somewhat taken aback by this, as he has been reading about how much, even in such an electronic era, people prefer face-to-face interaction, and how communication is much more effective when done like this. He agrees, however, to send her the document by email.

At the team meeting, she produces her tablet computer and, as the meeting progresses, she occasionally makes some notes electronically. The other team members watch for a while until one asks whether she had typed up the agenda herself (from the hard copy she had been given). On revealing that she had asked for it electronically rather than in hard copy, the other three team members say that had they known this was an option, they also would have preferred the electronic version. Peter is totally perplexed. Having by this stage read quite widely about communication in leadership, he finds that his actions seem to have had the opposite effect to that desired.

Commentary

This is not an unusual situation for a novice researcher to find themselves in, but it is one which can cause some anxiety. In the initial stages of an action research project, a researcher often finds difficulty with the grounded nature of the process. Additionally, the self-belief, and the patience required to 'let the data tell their own story', is, at a personal level difficult, and probably made much more so in the current quick-fix culture that exists in many schools or settings. The feeling of not knowing what is happening, of waiting until the path begins to make itself clear, can cause not only anxiety, but a feeling of incompetence. My own DPhil research diary records my own feelings on having done something similar. 'I don't think I'm cut out for this type of research at all – I just don't seem to recognise what's there in front of me.' As a more experienced researcher at the time, and having the luxury of a longer period of time in which to complete the study, I was able to take time to work through this feeling of incompetence, and to recognise it also as a helpful prompt for further reflection at a meta level. Peter, however, is in danger of feeling demotivated and asks his tutor for a meeting.

The wisdom and authority of established writers always seems more appealing, and more academically convincing, than an analysis of home-generated data from a small-scale project. There is an element here also of a 'dominant discourse' (already identified as a potential stumbling block in Chapter 2) in that Peter's willingness to be influenced by what he has read in the literature in relation to the importance of interpersonal relationships and face-to-face contact influences him more than the data he has generated.

Reflection

If you were Peter's tutor, how might you advise him to proceed now?

Methodological literature

This is an interesting body of literature, normally considered to be crucial at the preparatory stage of a project. For many researchers, it is the 'how to' of the project, and is read to provide some form of road map of the process. It may be incorporated into a 'methodology and design' section of a report and, on the whole, is considered as something to do early and be done with. New researchers may be cautioned by tutors about taking a basic road map or recipe approach to this literature, and advised that in the absence of developing a deep conceptual familiarity with the chosen methodological approach, it is possible to either design a project which lacks internal methodological consistency, or to use the research approach in a superficial way, unaware of its subtle philosophical nuances. Hammersley (2006) describes this as the 'methodology-as-technique' rather than the 'methodology-as-philosophy' approach. At various stages in this text, issues relating to our socialisation in a scientific concept of research and the power of a dominant discourse are discussed. As well as contributing to our misunderstanding of what action research can do, and our problems in accurately reading the data, they are also, and perhaps more fundamentally, indicative of a failure to fully embrace the underlying philosophy and epistemology in action research. While Hammersley cautions the counter-productivity of an approach which is entirely and therefore not usefully 'methodology-as-philosophy', he argues that 'philosophy is needed to clarify the value principles that educational researchers use to frame their inquiries'. It is perhaps in the exploration of these value principles and in consideration of their relevance to and meanings within the project that the methodological literature can have its greatest impact. Hutchinson and Whitehouse (1999: 153) suggest that not engaging with the underpinning philosophy, not addressing the values and beliefs implicit in action research can reduce it to a 'qualitative form of practical problem-solving'.

There can be pragmatic problems, too, in failing to engage in a conceptual way with appropriate methodological literature. Should a project subsequently not go as planned (which is a common occurrence in practitioner research of all types) the limitations of such an approach quickly become obvious. Without a philosophical underpinning, the 'gaps between theory and practice' (Carr, 1980: 63) become highly problematic.

These 'gaps' may be of two distinct types. The first represents a pragmatic or practical gap, the second a more philosophical one, although I would argue that, even in the first type, philosophical issues exist.

In the first instance, there is the relationship between the actions of a practitioner and his/her espoused theory of practice (although this may never have been an explicit theory of practice) which may expose some degree of 'mismatch'. This is often discovered by teachers researching and reflecting on their practice, and finding tensions between the values they claim to have and those that are evident in their practice. Whitehead (1993: 71) suggests that teachers using video-recordings of their teaching sessions will expose 'places where values are negated in practice'.

In the second instance, educational research may expose theory-practice gaps, if those who research practice have failed to recognise or realise the philosophical relationship between practice and theory, and hence use a 'methodology-as-technique' approach. Hammersley (2006: 274) describes this as taking an essentially 'experimental' view of methodology, ascribing to it a hierarchically superior position, and an understanding that, if applied correctly, it can produce 'virtually certain knowledge'.

It is my belief and my experience that the methodological literature is germane throughout the project. In fact, since action research is conceptualised as a holistic integration of theory and practice, of action and research, it would appear inconsistent to only consider the epistemological framework at the start of the project. Further, the literature of educational action research draws on questions about the nature and purpose of education, the values embodied in it, and the ways in which tensions between personal and organisational values may be manifest.

A short case example from my own DPhil study illustrates the importance of revisiting the methodological literature throughout the project. Having decided that my students needed more scope to undertake investigative work in science lessons, feeling that this would help them see science as a process of discovery, as well as one of rules and procedures, I recorded one of my teaching sessions in which I hoped to provide this opportunity. Guided by procedures for providing classroom investigations, I did not particularly question my approach, but simply justified it as meeting policy and practice requirements in my school, and genuinely believed that my students had a real opportunity to conduct an open-ended investigation.

Example

Analysis of the tape shows a teaching methodology contrary to that which I had believed I employed. The use of leading questions, interventions in discussions, and affirmation of the student who presented suggestions most closely matching the assessment criteria for the experiment, suggest that what Elliott (1997) described as educationally worthwhile autonomous thinking, was not a feature of the lesson at all. He defines educationally worthwhile activities in terms of value concepts such as critical thinking and learning through discovery or enquiry. They are evaluated in terms of the extent to which they intrinsically embody criteria and standards which are implicit in their educational ends. He quotes the example of students setting and posing questions about the subject matter as educationally worthwhile since it enacts the principle of enquiry learning as an educational end. On the other hand, the activity of the teacher asking leading questions is inconsistent with autonomous thinking, and therefore not educationally worthwhile.

It is interesting to note here that my analysis of practice was not informed by the substantive literature of science teaching, but by the methodological literature, discussing the concept of 'educationally worthwhile'. Appropriate for both the framing of the project and helpful for the interrogation of findings, it brought to my thinking an extra dimension that I believe would not have been precipitated by a reading of the substantive literature alone. It was, in essence, the continued reading of texts exploring the philosophical and conceptual underpinnings that began to shape my thinking as an action researcher. It was this continued engagement with such texts that allowed me to problematise my own practice and research findings within it. My continued reading of the methodological literature allowed me to ask better questions of the substantive matter of my study.

Eclectic literature

For many action researchers, myself included, a wide and eclectic range of literature has helped the sense-making process of the project. Little is written on this important subject, which can cause some vexation for less experienced researchers in particular. Why, for example, would the novels and poetry of the nineteenth century be acceptable as the literature in an action research project about physics teaching? How can an action researcher justify as theoretically sound the fact that reading a text on philosophy of science can make a contribution to their project on improving their own practice in supervising general action research projects?

In this section, I discuss the role of an eclectic literature in relation to these two (real) research projects, and explore how such an approach can be considered to be theoretically sound.

The first of the projects was my own DPhil study, exploring ways in which I, as a physics teacher, could make physics education more appealing to my students. A number of examples from this study used so far in this book have shown how I used a diary as a thinking and sense-making space, how I collected and collated data, and how I found myself confronted by the methodological literature during a data analysis stage of the study. This next section relates to the way in which some leisure reading suddenly became important to me and informed a further line of thought and interpretation.

The data from my project on girls in physics suggested that while the issues were not simply and exclusively gender based, there was a strong and complex gender issue throughout it. It became clear as I explored further, that the (UK) physics curriculum (and its implied pedagogy) drew heavily on values, beliefs and attitudes which had their origins in nineteenth century moves to professionalise both science and education. A reading of the history of science and the history of education clearly articulated the events of the period, but it was only on reading other texts that something of the social attitudes and values of the time clarified just what these events might mean and what their impact was. Rereading Jane Austen during a holiday, I had rather forcibly felt an emotional response to the place of women in society in the nineteenth century on reading the description of Mrs Goddard's school in *Emma*, 'a real, honest, old-fashioned Boarding school . . . where girls might be sent to be out of the way and scramble themselves into a little education, without any danger of coming back prodigies' (Austen, 1994: 17).

The impact on reading this, possibly heightened by the fact that I was relaxing, taking time away from my study, and thus not consciously thinking about it, was enormous. Having been reading about science and the professions in the late eighteenth and early nineteenth centuries, I had begun to have a reasonably clear picture of what life was like, and what constraints were placed on women. Somehow, though, I had understood what I had read as 'behaviours' rather than emotional and emotive articulations of belief and value. The very language in that short quotation from Emma ('sent to be out of the way', and 'scramble themselves into a little education') trivialised the education process (as it pertained to young women) but, more importantly, trivialised women themselves. The emotional response that I had, and the connection I made to my reading of the more substantive, and historical, literature encouraged me to read novels and poetry from the eighteenth and nineteenth centuries to try to assimilate and understand their culture more fully.

Discovering Maria Edgeworth provided a powerful insight into the ways in which even educated women were located within society. At the start of the century, Edgeworth (Edgeworth and Edgeworth, 1798: 550) had warned that a woman's 'imagination must not be raised above the taste for necessary occupations, or the numerous small, but not trifling pleasures of domestic life'. During the nineteenth century, education had evolved to fit a woman to fulfil these duties.

Likewise, in an era when plant reproduction was discussed in moral and lawful terms (bridal beds of flower petals was an analogy used to give propriety to their reproductive behaviour), biologically allegorical poetry was written to decry the behaviour of libertine (usually academic) women:

Bath'd in new bliss, the Fair-one greets the bower

And ravishes a flame from every flower. (Polwhele, 1800, cited in Benjamin, 1991: 33–4)

The very title of the poem, 'The Unsex'd Females', refers to women lacking the qualities deemed appropriate to the female sex. It was reading literature such as this that challenged me to read beyond the descriptive as I read accounts of the genesis of professional education and science. Indeed, I would contest, that it was *only* through such reading that I became able to fully appreciate the nuances in historical accounts, and the implications they had. Thus, while much of my reading drew on what might be called an 'appropriate' body of literature, it was perhaps through my somewhat eclectic approach that real clarity in my thinking developed. My emotional response to such literature played no small part in its impact on my more rational understanding, reminding me that, as Reason and Torbet (2001: 7) claim, 'all knowing is based in the feeling, thinking, attending experiential presence of persons in their world'.

The second of the two projects relates to a PhD study conducted by the late Kath Green. Finding herself starting the project from an open-ended exploratory stance, she felt that it was important that she 'avoided adopting precisely this predetermined type of approach in relation to defining the field of literature that might best inform my inquiry' (Green, 1999: 108). She was conscious that only on having read a significant quantity of literature would she be in a position to identify its relevance to her. It is interesting to see how she defines relevance in this case. Taking an intensely personal approach to it, she says 'I wanted to report on the literature that had really made a difference to my thinking.' (Green, 1999: 110). In her article, she goes on to describe how the philosophy of chaos theory in science helped her understand her own complex and often chaotic field of enquiry. Likewise, her reading around the butterfly effect helps her understand the sensitivities within her enquiry, and the ways in which small changes in her own thinking in one small part of her work may send ripples through the whole study.

Cogently illustrating the importance of literature from outside either the substantive or methodological field, Green states that 'I would want to argue that good action research *demands* that we show a willingness to step outside our usual frames of reference, that we question our habitual ways of seeing and that we constantly seek out fresh perspectives on the familiar' (1999: 121, emphasis in original).

A particular resonance for me is the way in which she sees the relationship between aspects of her practice, and indicating that while at times she might want to 'zoom in' on individual aspects, she keeps returning to a full picture in order to see relationship, to see her practice in its wholeness. She quotes Briggs's work on fractals to explain what she meant: 'dynamical systems imply a holism in which everything influences, or potentially influences, everything else – because everything is in some sense constantly interacting with everything else' (Briggs, 1992: 21).

From my own perspective, this very elegantly sums up not just the relationships that exist within practice, but also, in an action research project, that reciprocity between action and research. Indeed, it would suggest that in an action research project, there should and could be no separation of 'the literature' into categories of any sort. Green suggests something of this as she considers the perceptions others may have of this definition of, and engagement with, the literature. She suggests that this approach could be seen as intellectually unsound, lacking in rigour and having something of a 'pick and mix' nature to it. It is at this stage that I feel she demonstrates most effectively the way in which such perceived randomism may be justified and, if necessary, assessed. Suggesting that reading a list of references is not sufficient to assess whether or not the chosen literature is appropriate, she argues that decisions about its adequacy 'can only be made in light of *the use made of it*' (Green, 1999: 122, emphasis in original).

She draws the threads of her argument together by saying:

> Knowledge about our practice as teachers is something we construct rather than find and it cuts across traditional disciplinary boundaries. It seems to me that action research would be strengthened by encouraging researchers to draw on *any* literature that supports them in seeing their practice with fresh eyes, in challenging the assumptions they bring to their practice, and in helping them to both articulate and critique the values they bring to their practice. (1999: 123, emphasis in original)

Making effective use of the literature

What to read

Whenever and however the literature is chosen, it is important that it is done in a way which brings criticality and clarity to the research. Interestingly, I have sometimes found that the traditional literature review can fail to do this. Anxious to demonstrate that they have read a good selection of appropriate and relevant texts, the researcher may then go on to write the literature chapter as an inventory of what has been read, and what information has been gleaned from it.

Stark (1998) cautions against approaches such as the 'magpie' approach (whereby seemingly interesting articles are collected and accessed, even those not directly relevant to the study), the 'diamond necklace' approach (consisting of a string of quotations from well-known authors, and little in the way of linking or conversational commentary) and the 'dressed to impress' approach (in which a bibliography, rather than a reference list, is presented, with few of the books or titles informing discussion in the text of the work). She advocates a list of questions that the reader might ask when reading in order that they can more fully engage with the arguments and counter-arguments presented. In particular, she cautions researchers to ensure that they recognise the particular stance or standpoint of an author or source. This is a particularly important consideration when undertaking practice-based research. Many practitioners will already be quite familiar with policy in their field of work, and will find a range of official publications helpful in understanding their research. However, this can provide a somewhat one-sided view, and it will be necessary to read a range of other sources so that, as Green (1999) advocates, they are helped to see their practice with fresh eyes, and challenge their assumptions. In a study of teaching and learning in young children, it will be necessary to read perspectives from philosophy, psychology and/or sociology, children's story books, games and toys may also, however, provide rich insights.

In addition to the subject matter of the texts read, there must also be some consideration given to their nature. Are they research papers? Textbooks? Web sources? Knowing their nature is helpful in relation to helping understand their potential for informing the research project.

The classificatory system provided by Thomas (2009: 32–4) is particularly helpful in explaining the strengths and weakness of each source, providing an insight into how and why each type of source is as it is. A particularly hard to read article, for example, may be so because it is published in a high-stakes, highly specialised, peer-reviewed journal and, as such, its intended audience is a particular section of the academic community. Conversely, a more accessible article, published by a practitioner in a professional journal, may be based on a less rigorous study, and present findings of questionable validity. There may be few references to other work in the field, and little development of theoretical perspectives. As a reader, you need to interrogate each source carefully in order to assess its usefulness to the project, and its integrity.

The use of websites as a source of literature and theoretical perspectives is widespread, but sometimes confusing for researchers. It used to be considered in some academic circles as the poor relation in terms of literature sources, but it has become increasingly accepted as a legitimate source of valid information. However, given the quantity of information available in this way, it is to be expected that the quality is variable. For this reason, the assessment of quality can be a particular challenge. There are, however, many sites hosted by known and respected authors in the field. Jean McNiff (www.jeanmcniff.com), Jack Whitehead (www.action research.net) and Bob Dick (www.aral.com.au) are just three examples of known academics who share much of their work openly via their website. Likewise, university faculties and research centres such as the Centre for Collaborative Action Research at Pepperdine University (http://cadres. pepperdine.edu/ccar/about.html), the Centre for Practitioner Research at National-Louis University (http://www.nl.edu/cfpr/resources/websites. cfm) and the Economic and Social Research Council (ESRC)-funded Teaching and Learning Research Programme (http://www.tlrp.org) provide both resources and links to other sites. In general, materials accessed via these sites and portals will be of good quality, although as before, they will need to be read in the knowledge of the author's particular stance.

In general, reading a wide range of materials from a good variety of source types provides you with a more balanced view of the field. Seeing a range of personal viewpoints can help you to recognise and articulate your own views (something that is not always clearly articulated by a researcher in their work). Engaging with a range of perspectives (personal and otherwise) will help you develop your own analysis and evaluation skills. Reading particular pieces will introduce new ideas, and provide you with links to further reading.

As a final word in terms of 'what to read', you will come across books that are summaries of other work or fairly general in their focus. In relation to the methodological literature, you will see general texts on doing research projects which can provide an excellent introduction to, and overview of, the field. Having been introduced though, reading either primary sources or more specific texts will help you better understand the nature of your chosen methodology. Likewise, a general text on leadership and management might be a useful starting point, but a more specific text dealing with the management of transition will give deeper insights in a change management project. While the appropriate choice of reading materials is a major consideration in a project, the way in which they are read is equally important.

How to read

It has not been unusual in my experience to see a literature review chapter neither introduced nor concluded with any text to connect it to the enquiry in question. Occasionally, it is also difficult to infer any connection. I find myself wondering just what the engagement with the materials was, why this particular body of literature was chosen and what, if any, has been the impact on the researcher's thinking.

Poulson and Wallace, (2004) treat reading and writing as two sides of a coin in a way that I think is really helpful for anyone engaged in research. Given that it is common to present the report in the form of a written document (but see Chapter 8 for other possibilities), any reading done will inform the writing of the report. Outlining the relationship between the thought processes involved in both reading and writing, they present them in a comparative table (Figure 5.1).

Table 5.1   Critically reading, critically writing

As a critical reader of the literature, you:	As a self-critical writer of the literature, you:
Consider the authors' purpose in writing the account	State your purpose in what you write to make it clear to your readers
Examine the structure of the account to help you understand how the authors develop their argument	Create a logical structure for your account that assists you with developing your argument, and make it clear to your readers
Seek to identify the main claims the authors make in putting forward their argument	State your own main claims clearly to help your readers understand your argument
Adopt a sceptical stance towards the authors' claims, checking whether they support convincingly what they assert	Assume that your readers adopt a sceptical stance to your work, so you must convince them by supporting your claims as far as possible
Question whether the authors have sufficient backing for the generalisations they make	Avoid making sweeping generalisations in your writing which you cannot justify to your readers
Check what the authors mean by key terms in the account and whether they use these terms consistently	Define the key terms you employ in your account so that your readers are clear what you mean, and use these terms consistently
Consider whether and how any values guiding the authors' work may affect what they claim	Make explicit any values that guide what you write
Distinguish between respecting the authors as people and being sceptical about what they write	Avoid attacking authors as people but are sceptical about what they write
Keep an open mind, retaining a conditional willingness to be convinced	Assume that your readers are open-minded about your work and are willing to be convinced if you can adequately support your claims

As a critical reader of the literature, you:	As a self-critical writer of the literature, you:
Check that everything the authors have written is relevant to their purpose in writing the account and the argument they develop	Sustain your focus throughout your account, and avoid irrelevancies and digressions in what you write
Expect to be given the information that is needed for you to be in a position to check any other literature sources to which the authors refer	Ensure that your referencing in the text and the reference list is complete and accurate so that your readers are in a position to check your sources

Source: Poulson and Wallace (2004: 7)

I have found it helpful to encourage my students to reconstruct the statements in each category as questions to be used as prompts for self-reflection. In what way, for example, do they 'adopt a sceptical stance towards the authors' claims, checking whether they support convincingly what they assert'? To what extent do they 'consider whether and how any values guiding the authors' work may affect what they claim'?

Reflection

When you are undertaking you reading, (how) do you ensure that you engage with it in a sceptical way? How do you ensure that you can keep your mind open to finding sources which at first may not have seemed directly relevant?

Summary

In this chapter we have explored some of the ways in which you can locate, read and review, and engage with a wide range of literature for your project. While there are differences of opinion in relation to when and how the literature should be used in an action research project, there is still a common understanding that it should be wide in range and scope, come from a range of types of sources and, most importantly, be engaged with in a way that challenges. Its purpose is not only to show that you know what has already been written, but to show how it has informed and possibly changed your thinking.

Further reading

Green, K. (1999) 'Defining the field of literature in action research: a personal approach', *Educational Action Research*, 7(1): 105–24.

This highly accessible paper outlines both the narrative and the analysis of Kath Green's own engagement with the literature in relation to her action research study. Her approach, and in particular the way in which she retains an open mind as to what will prove useful in helping her own thinking, is one which I have found helpful to many students.

Davies, J. (2007) 'Rethinking the architecture: an action researcher's resolution to writing and presenting their thesis', *Action Research*, 5(2): 181–98.

This paper presents a highly personal and well-argued justification for a less conventional written account of action research. Davies clearly justifies the way in which her chosen representation suits both the process of the research project as well as providing a clear structure for reporting its outcomes. She also shows very clearly how her use of the literature was a continuous process, informing her thinking at every stage, and thus not appropriately written as a separate 'literature review' section.

 Additional online resources can be found at:
www.sagepub.co.uk/beraseries.sp

CHAPTER 6

USING DATA: MAKING SENSE AND MAKING CLAIMS

One of the most important outcomes of any piece of research is the claim that it makes to knowledge, insight or understanding. In many cases this is the public, and only, face of the research process. Most of us will be familiar with the type of advertising that relies on 'research studies', and their efficacy in improving sales figures is testament to the way in which we almost unquestioningly believe information based on 'research'. It is often only when discussion and debate around research outcomes becomes a matter of public interest that we begin to ask questions about the research process itself, how it was designed, what data were actually produced and how the claims made relate to that data. In recent years, issues such as cloning, genetic engineering, and children's vaccination programmes have all come under public scrutiny not only in relation to sensationalised headlining of research findings, but also in relation to the design of the research project, the data collected and their interpretation.

Chapter 4 dealt with matters relating to the presentation and analysis of data, outlining ways in which sense can be made of the unstructured and qualitative types of data that an action research project can generate. In this chapter we develop how, having analysed and identified themes, we can then begin to understand how this sense-making process contributes to knowledge generation. How can we make defensible knowledge claims on the basis of our findings? We can start by further exploring the sense-making process itself, identifying ways in which we can do it assiduously and authentically that also demonstrates academic integrity. From this we can then explore the various research quality indicators that exist, and discuss their applicability to action research projects.

Research findings: making sense

In Chapter 4, we began to explore some of the sources of data in an action research project, some approaches to their collection, collation and presentation. In particular, the important but complex task of thoroughly analysing unstructured and text-based data was introduced as a process of *thematic analysis*. This skill is a lynchpin in the armoury of any action researcher and owes much to the work of theorists such as Strauss and Corbin (1990) and Miles and Huberman (1994), among others. Based on the concept of grounded theory, the thematic analysis of free-response data allows the researcher to generate theory from data, rather than apply theory to practice, or test practice against theory. For many practitioner-researchers, this is a powerful, and even empowering approach, which provides the impetus to action that is implicit in action research.

In practice, a researcher at this stage in a project will need to become closely conversant with, or immersed in, the data and on the basis of this, start a *coding* process through which key points from the data can be identified throughout the set. Chapter 4 outlines some guidance in this, enabling the researcher to develop *concepts*, then *categories* and finally *theory*. Some practical steps that might be taken include:

• Closely examining each data source or set and, from first reading, identify any points which seem to be emerging (and, if appropriate, their strength)
• Identifying any points of agreement between the various sources or perspectives. Consider how these points of agreement might relate to the

initial research question. These confirmatory findings can help build the explanatory theory of practice.

- Carefully and thoroughly searching the data sets for points of disagreement. These points are perhaps even more important than points of agreement, as they highlight areas of possible incomplete understanding. They are usually triggers for exploration or data collection, and in being disconfirmational, allow the researcher to test their emerging understanding.
- Identifying any unexpected data. It is not uncommon in research of this type for the researcher to be surprised by some of the findings. While many researchers will try to take a grounded theory, or theory-building, approach which should be theory-neutral at the outset, it is unlikely that some explanatory theory is not present. Even if not articulated, the element of surprise at some findings suggests that it is present at a subliminal level. As such, then, it is not unusual to find some data which challenge this subliminal theory.

The following case study presents a set of data from a study conducted by Khalil, a university tutor exploring participants' perceptions of the relevance of their professional development programme.

Case study

Khalil is a tutor in a university who leads a continuing professional development (CPD) programme for teachers. Charged with updating the programme in a way that ensures its relevance to teachers, he undertakes the process as an action research project. He asks, 'How can I improve my practice as CPD tutor so that my programme better suits the needs of teachers?' He starts this process by designing a questionnaire to glean from his current cohort of teacher participants the reasons that have prompted them to undertake the programme. The respondents come from a number of specialist areas within the CPD programme. He collates the following responses to the question 'What was your main reason for undertaking CPD?':

- To inform and develop teaching skills and knowledge.
- To further my career and pursue interests.

(Continued)

(Continued)

- I am aiming for MA and assistance with promotion.
- To improve career prospects.
- To improve chances of crossing the threshold (a measured level of competence in the UK which brings increased pay when successfully 'crossed').
- To enhance my understanding of educational management.
- To be aware of current good practice.
- To help develop my knowledge of mentoring.
- To gain a higher degree for job promotion.
- To gain a qualification in specialism.
- Needed a new challenge.
- Pure interest in learning, and career development.
- To enhance my qualifications/research interests.
- Had to – employer policy.
- Continuation of studies, following on from NPQH. (NPQH is the National Professional Qualification for Headship, in the UK.)
- An interest in pursuing academic research.
- Post-threshold performance management.
- Interest in subject, and in meeting other teachers during career break.
- To return to the classroom after a career break.
- For personal growth, pleasure and accreditation.
- To learn more about classroom/pupil–teacher interaction.
- To develop my learning in the field of e-learning pedagogy.
- The chance to take an MA at a heavily subsidised cost.
- Lots of staff in our school already have an MA, didn't want to be left behind.

He decides that the best way in which to begin his analysis is to physically place the statements (each on a separate piece of paper) in separate piles, adding to each as he considers the way in which the set is constituted. After some time, he has the following sets:

- Career development
- Subject/other specific knowledge
- Intellectual challenge and growth
- Financial reasons.

> ## Reflection
>
>
>
> Make your own headings under which you could sort these statements. (Do you agree with Khalil's?) How might you categorise these two statements? 'The chance to take an MA at a heavily subsidised cost' and 'Financial reasons'?

Commentary

Khalil uses his initial codification process to help him not only in the preliminary analysis of his questionnaire data, but also to compare and contrast with the responses from his other two open-ended questions:

1 What benefits have you seen from engaging with the programme?
2 How do you think the programme could be improved?

He hopes in this way to begin to understand why it is that the teachers signed up for the CPD programme, how they have benefited from it and how they feel it could be improved. He hopes also to develop an overall sense of what it is that motivates teachers to undertake such programmes and, having done so, remain on them. From this sense, he will be able to further develop his analysis; the key concepts and categories will guide him to further thinking and reading so that he will begin to know not just what the data seem to say, but also what it might mean in a wider sense. He thus develops his own explanatory theory of his practice, and also explores the relationship of his personal theory to larger theoretical constructs. This is a vital element in the business of making knowledge claims. While it is normally the case that practitioner-researchers use the concept of 'theorising practice' to mean well-developed reflection on practice, and the development of explanatory models and devices, the claim to knowledge should also explore the relationship to the wider theoretical field, interrogating and conversing with already existing bodies of knowledge. In Khalil's case, his question relating to how the programme might be developed could provide data about how his course participants best engage in their professional learning and, hence, his further reading might be around theories of androgogy.

Reflection

Look at the sets compiled by Khalil, and suggest how he might direct his broader reading to enable him to use his own emerging understanding in a way that relates to broader theory in the field. What type of texts would you advise him to search for?

Quality matters

Throughout the sense-making process, and the further analyses (and, indeed, throughout all aspects of the project) it is crucial that appropriate quality processes are in place. Debates around appropriate quality indicators are evident in numerous texts, and range from the perspective of authors such as Carr and Elliott writing in the 1980s and 1990s, to the re-articulation and renaming of quality indicators in recent years by Saunders (2007), Feldman (2007) and others.

Elliott (1997) suggests that educational practice embodies its own inherent criteria and standards which are morally determined and embodied in the ends of education. Thus, quality indicators are an intrinsic property of a properly constituted educational practice and, as such, cannot be named in a generally and broadly applicable way. Heikkinen et al. (2007) provide more of a renaming, and suggest that as a fundamentally narrative process, action research should demonstrate historical continuity, reflexivity, dialectics, workability and evocativeness as its quality indicators. These criteria are not proposed as mutually exclusive, nor are they proposed as a checklist, but are presented as the product of the authors' own experiences in supervising, reading and supporting action research projects.

Many texts on research methods will have a chapter or section dealing with quality indicators where words like reliability, validity, replicability, objectivity, generalisability and so forth will often feature as key criteria against which to assess the quality of the work. These criteria may, at first, seem appropriate to you as you read them. They are, after all, familiar terms and concepts, and sit well with our instinctive understanding of research. You may, however, as you become more engaged in your project, start to find them conceptually rather incongruent. How, for example, can you be 'objective' in an action research project? Why might you want to be? Chapter 3 touches on something of this paradigmatic inconsistency, citing the work of Oancea and Furlong (2007) who caution that concepts of 'good' are situated concepts, and will vary from one paradigm to another. Rather than identify key quality indicators, they suggest four categories through which paradigm-specific indicators can be articulated: trustworthiness, contribution to knowledge, transparency and explicitness in design and reporting, and paradigmatic considerations (Oancea and Furlong, 2007: 128).

Let us consider, for example, 'trustworthiness'. In some types of research this may legitimately be demonstrated by showing both validity and reliability of the research tools. If we are assessing the extent to which a particular procedure can be guaranteed to produce a valid outcome (that is, do what it is supposed to do) time and time again, then the concepts of validity and reliability are vital in ensuring quality. If, however, we are assessing the narrative account of someone's personal and professional development over a period of time, then the concepts are meaningless. Heikkinen et al.'s (2007) notions of historical continuity, reflexivity and evocativeness would seem much more aligned to and consistent with the work being evaluated, and effectively demonstrate 'trustworthiness'.

Dana's (2009) approach to quality indicators is similar in some respects to that of Oancea and Furlong, in that it invites contextualised response to general headings. Identifying five key headings, action researchers respond with the ways in which these criteria have been understood and met within their own study:

- *Context of study* (in which the writer attempts to give the reader a clear understanding of the setting and context in which the research took place)
- *Wonderings and purpose* (in which the writer provides the reader with a justification and root of the 'wonderings' that initiated the project, and the intellectual and reflective relevance of it)
- *Principal research design (data collection and data analysis)* (in which the writer describes the multiple sources to be used in the project, and the data collection strategy, procedure, timeline, and data analysis are clearly explained)
- *Principal-researcher learning* (while her text was written for principal teacher researchers in the USA, this criterion can be adapted for any researcher as the way in which they articulate their personal and professional learning gained from undertaking the study)
- *Implications for practice* (which enable the writer to articulate both the changes in practice that have been part of the enquiry, and also further possibilities for change).

Feldman (2007: 30) produces a similar set of criteria to those above, suggesting that all research reports should include:

- clear and detailed descriptions of how and why data were collected
- clear and detailed descriptions of how their narratives were constructed from the data
- multiple perspectives, remembering to 'use them to critique the views that one holds'
- an explanation of why the actions led to the results.

Bringing a clear imperative to explain, I feel that these criteria together enable the researcher to move beyond the position of 'application of quality criteria' (even though done in a narrative manner) to one of justification.

Quality words

Reason and Bradbury (2006) capture some of the essence of this debate in raising the matter of vocabulary. Citing Kvale's questioning of the validity of the term 'validity' in a discourse which is significantly different from that in which the term originates, and Schwandt's naming of the application of uniform measures as 'criteriology', they question not only the vocabulary used, but the underlying philosophy which it articulates. In contributing to what they cite Lather (1993) identifying as 'the fertile obsession with validity', and seek to 'broaden the bandwidth' of concerns around 'what constitutes good research/practice'. In this way, they hope that a 'shared, and no doubt growing vocabulary providing clarity about common ground and disagreement can only improve both the quality of our work and collegial relationships in action research' (Reason and Bradbury, 2006: 343). They identify five particular choice points in the action research project as places or issues in the research at which conversations should be had about the worth of the research. Identifying relationships, practical outcomes, extended ways of knowing, purpose and enduring consequences, they challenge the action researcher to question whether or not their work actually is about 'getting valuable work done well' (ibid).

Quality work

'Getting valuable work done well' provides us with an additional dimension to the concept of quality in action research. Action research is the only research approach whose primary purpose is to improve practice, and it is fitting that improvement in practice should play some part in the assessment of quality in the process. How, then, can we relate the concept of 'quality' to changes in practice? This becomes a bifurcated and potentially diversionary question, in that it may be suggestive of a low-level evaluation of a specific implementation. Bridges (2007) talks of the erosion of teacher professionalism in the UK through successive changes in the central prescription of all matters relating to education, suggesting that we have moved 'From Profession to Trade' through what he calls 'the marketisation of education' (Bridges, 2007: 454). Citing Powers (1993) he discusses 'New Bureaucracy of Audit and the "Pathologicality of Checking"' (2007: 455) and describes the dominance of a changing view of 'quality assurance' that stifles creativity in teaching and learning. Thus, asking a question about the improvement in practice brought about by an action research project can, in such an environment, be interpreted as a question about standards and competencies, rather than, as Bridges suggests, questions relating to the 'teacher's own authentic conviction as to the worthwhileness of what is being taught and the appropriateness, including the moral acceptability, of the way in which it is taught' (2007: 457). In essence, he is highlighting action research, in its deeply personal reflection on practice, on values and beliefs, as one way of redressing the balance. Suggesting that 'at its best, classroom action research seems to me to represent a reaffirmation of professional integrity, responsibility and authority in an environment that threatens to undermine all of these' (2007: 458), Bridges clearly challenges us all to define our notions of 'quality' in a way that meets the needs of education based on honesty and openness. He cautions that to do this is not easy when the educational system has suffered a sustained and systematic erosion of the intellectual pillars of critical engagement with policy and practice. However, despite his cautionary note, he believes action research can bring the concept of quality back into education, and the continuing numbers of teachers and other practitioners willing to engage in action research are testament to this.

If we thus define quality in improved practice in a way that is aligned more to beliefs and values than to competencies and external criteria, it should relate to the ways in which the thoughtful teacher can (re)align his or her practice to believe in its worthwhileness. Attard (2012), in discussing his own 'reflective odyssey', gives some indication of how this (re)alignment might be supported. He describes the process of reflective writing as a key mechanism through which he develops his understanding of his practice, explores the theory–practice relationship, and formulates strategies for improvement, saying, 'I start thinking critically about my past actions and how these together with educational theory can inform future practice'. Through the explication of his personal theories and tacit knowledge he discusses the 'need to unlearn taken-for-granted assumptions', suggesting that through this he can 'understand how prior learning and inherited values affect [my] professional practice and professional development' (Attard, 2012: 164). In effect, he is suggesting that the quality of his (self-study, reflective) research is inextricably linked to his willingness to write sometimes difficult reflective narratives and subject them to ongoing review and what he describes as 'conversing with oneself' (2012: 166).

Making appropriate choices

As a researcher, one of your primary roles is to ensure rigour in your work. Whether you choose to use the language of positivistic paradigms, or the more interpretist language of the mediation and construction of truth, multiple truths, authenticity or practice development, you need to ensure that it is chosen in a way that is appropriate for, and congruent with, the research question asked and the research approach chosen. Demonstration of this congruity is, in itself, an indicator of quality.

Let us return to the practical problem facing researchers as they begin to analyse an initial data set. We have already seen Cain (2011) discuss how it is possible to be swayed more by the authority of published work than your own data, thus producing an interpretation that is not true to the data. It is also possible that such misinterpretation can be caused by the dominance of a particular culture or discourse.

The dominant discourse

As human beings, culturally and socially located in our world, we are inevitably susceptible to the dominant discourse. By this I mean that modes of discourse become so culturally embedded that they enter into widespread acceptance, and are rarely the subject of question or debate. Normally created by those in power, it will contain particular ideological beliefs and quickly become the accepted way of seeing things. Over time, it not only becomes the way in which we hear things, but also the way in which we speak and think about those same things. (This is an effect of the situation presented earlier in which Bridges (2007) discusses centrally legislated changes and their impact on the operation of schools.) We adopt both a language and a philosophy congruent with it. To challenge the discourse is to challenge both the ideology and the power base. In the context of education, any teacher with a number of years' experience will be able to easily recall and document the evolving language of schools over a period of years. Some further reflection will reveal the parallel evolution of underpinning philosophy. An interesting exploration in this regard is the changing terminology surrounding those children with special or additional learning needs. Language which was deemed acceptable 20 years ago, may now be no longer approved of Corresponding to, and parallel with, this change in language there has also been a change in provision and attitudes. Likewise, the changing language of schools and their place in the community reveals changing structures and attitudes in school leadership and public accountability. Teachers nowadays speak in a language that is significantly different from that of schools and classrooms 30 years ago. We do not, however, usually compare and contrast them. We operate in current systems, and for the most part come to accept their legitimacy. In many ways, current ideologies and their associated discourses become our 'motherhood and apple pie'.

While this may be appropriate in many respects, and is a pragmatic necessity on the whole, it can hold a significant problem for the researcher. The power of the dominant discourse can impact significantly on the ability to analyse research data effectively. Susan's story provides one such example.

The seduction of the dominant discourse

Susan's story, part 1

In the mid-1990s, Susan was a teacher of English literature in a secondary school. Ten years into her teaching career she was finding that her GCSE group was proving to be rather challenging. Although the class group did not have a track record of behaving badly in general, she found that when they were in her lessons they lacked motivation, rarely had done any preparatory homework, and were easily distracted. There appeared to her to be an air of non-engagement in the classroom, and their academic progress was not quite what was expected. She felt that although she was not having major problems with the class, something was 'not quite right', and could be improved. In essence, she had the typical starting point of an action research project, and used this as a focus for her postgraduate professional development programme at university.

She began the reconnaissance phase by giving the group a questionnaire. It was designed to do two things. First, she wanted to establish the scale of the 'problem', and so elected to present 10 closed questions requiring scaled responses. She hoped that, if carefully designed, they would provide her with some indication of how many students in the class were in some way disengaged. Secondly, she wished to establish the nature of the problem. What exactly could she find out about their response to her classes? To address this, she then added two open items in the form of sentence completion activities. Pupils were asked to complete each of the two sentences, using them to explain what they enjoyed and did not enjoy about English literature classes. These two activities, items 11 and 12, asked students to complete each of the following two sentences:

11   I enjoy English literature because . . .
12   I do not enjoy English literature because . . .

She noted that some questions were not answered by all students, while other questions had more than one response from an individual. Nevertheless, she felt that the information would help inform her thinking.

Table 6.1 outlines the closed-response questions and a summary of the responses from her group of 26 students.

Table 6.1   Responses to English Literature questionnaire

Item	Strongly disagree	Disagree	Neutral	Agree	Strongly agree
1 English literature is usually an interesting lesson	3	11	5	2	2
2 I enjoy the novel that we are studying for GCSE	9	8	3	5	1
3 The pace of English literature lessons is too fast	0	3	10	5	8
4 It is interesting to read plays	14	8	2	1	1
5 I like the selection of poetry that we have been reading	16	6	2	3	0
6 The pace of lessons is mostly 'just right'	12	8	4	1	2
7 We do interesting activities in lessons	10	0	0	0	3
9 The structure of lessons is helpful	3	4	14	3	2
10 I would like to study English literature for A level	13	7	4	1	1

Reflection

Note the similarities in the design of Khalil's and Susan's projects. Do you think the design is effective? If so, how and in what way? If not, how and in what way, and what would make it better?

Commentary

Susan hopes that this information, alongside the responses from the two open-response questions will help her initial analysis so that she can use Elliott's (1991) model to form action hypotheses, and from these formulate action steps. She has collated her results into the table, and collected a set of responses to the two open response items. It is important for her to get this initial analysis 'right', as it provides the foundation on which she will base her action hypotheses and the resulting action steps. Implementing these steps will help her test and refine her initial understanding and analysis of the problem.

Reflection

1 Review the information presented in relation to items 1–10 on Susan's questionnaire and, on the basis of your reading and analysis of it, write a paragraph summarising and reporting on her findings.
2 Consider the range of responses that may have been obtained for items 11 and 12 on the questionnaire, and consider a means by which Susan could collate and analyse them.

Commentary

The purpose of the data analysis stage is to help make data-based or data-derived claims to knowing. In moving from raw data to data description, through to analysis and interpretation, the researcher is undergoing the process of sense-making and, through further connection with existing theory, starting to build new knowledge. The analysis of qualitative data is complex, and in Susan's case, the use of a tightly structured questionnaire with closed-response items is, in itself, an initial form of analysis. For this reason, as well as for others discussed in Chapter 4, the quality of the questionnaire design is of vital importance.

However, it is in the two free-response questions that the main business of analysis begins. Given that even in such a small-scale study as this one, 26 completely free responses will have been given to each of items 11 and 12, there needs to be a considered and consistent approach to producing analysis. As is the case throughout action research, a return to the initial focus is vital in helping make choices. What is it that these questions were meant to uncover? In the case of Susan's project, she was trying to find out what the students actually thought of English literature lessons. For this reason, a *thematic analysis* of the data is appropriate, which you might like to bear in mind as we progress through discussion of Susan's project. Her identified themes will be key in supporting her claims to knowing.

Susan's story, part 2

Susan collates the responses to items 11 and 12, many of which indicate that they enjoy English literature because 'it's better than maths', 'last lesson on Friday, and the weekend is starting', with only two properly positive

(Continued)

(Continued)

responses suggesting that 'it's good to read interesting books', and 'I've always enjoyed reading'. Responses to item 12 suggest that when they do not enjoy English literature, they use words and phrases such as: 'hard', 'boring' 'lessons are dull', 'too much reading', 'too much writing', 'too many hard words', 'stupid poems', 'boring books' and similar comments. One pupil did not complete this item, saying that they 'really liked and enjoyed it'.

On the basis of this, and her analysis of the closed-response items (Table 6.1), Susan moves through the formulation of action hypotheses and action plans to prepare to implement, monitor and evaluate her main action step in the hope that at the end of a six-week period, she will notice and be able to evidence a difference in the class group's attitude.

Reflection

Review the data presented in Table 6.1, and along with the brief further information you have seen in part 2 of the case study, consider what initial action hypotheses Susan might draw up, and what initial action steps she might consider.

Susan's story, part 3

Susan approaches the ICT department in the school, and negotiates a six-week period during which she can have access to a dedicated ICT room for one lesson each week. At the same time, she plans lessons which allow pupils to do some of their written work using computers, and plans access to some Internet sites which provide structured activities in response to the texts they are required to read.

Commentary

In reflecting on Susan's story, it must be remembered that it has its origins some years ago, when the use of technology in schools was very much a topic of conversation. In the 1990s, many schools had one or two dedicated ICT rooms, and the more forward-thinking may have had a single computer for teacher use in classrooms. Interactive whiteboards had not arrived and, on the whole, computers that were available in classrooms, did not usually have Internet access. Despite this, it was a period when ICT was sold as the panacea to all ills in classrooms. Almost every statement of special needs issued to an assessed child suggested that a laptop computer would make a very positive improvement. Whether the problem was low self-esteem, dyslexia, dyspraxia or ADHD, the answer always seemed to incorporate ICT. In other words, the ICT agenda was very prominent, promoting a particular belief in what ICT might be able to do, and it became a dominant discourse in schools and classrooms. Teachers were encouraged to explore ways in which they could integrate it into their teaching, and not to do so was seen as being (unreasonably) resistant to change.

The case study therefore provides us with a powerful example of what a dominant discourse is, and how it impacts on our thinking. Despite a body of evidence telling her that pupils found the subject hard and dull, requiring them to read books they disliked and had little interest in, the seduction of the dominant ICT discourse suggests to Susan that ICT is the most appropriate response to her situation. Although the study may appear somewhat outdated, the principle remains the same today. As discussed earlier, we live in the present, and on the whole assimilate its norms, values and cultures. Dominant discourses make their way into our language, our thought processes and our way of being in the world. Such is their power, that they can go unrecognised. In going unrecognised, they also go unchallenged. In Susan's case, it was through discussing her project with her university tutor and course colleagues that she realised the mismatch between her data set and her analysis. Through failing to see, and therefore challenge, how her world view was colouring her interpretation of data, she was failing to produce a valid outcome from her findings. The use of other voices as critical friends in the process, bringing the clarity of distance from the project, helped Susan identify, and thus question, her assumptions and early analysis. Reflecting on the earlier discussions on concepts of quality, we can also see that Susan was in danger of not being able to substantiate any claims to knowledge she might make about her practice, and was unlikely to implement action steps which would make the desired improvement.

Reflection

Consider the ways in which your practice is shaped and guided by political and other discourses. Can you identify any in particular that have become normalised? How might you both identify and challenge them in your own action research projects?

One option that Susan could have explored was a process for 'checking' her own interpretation through the use of a validation group. McNiff (2002) describes this as a set of people who could make professional judgements about the validity and authenticity of a report and give critical feedback. The addition of their voice can add a fresh insight to the process, providing the slightly distanced view of the 'intelligent outsider'.

Another perspective that she could have sought was that of her own pupils. Asking them 'Is this a valid conclusion from what you told me?' would have allowed her not only to address the validity of her interpretation, but also would have allowed the pupils to work in a democratic way with her, co-constructing meaning and understanding. The conversation itself could have provided a further data set for her study. This process of data validation addresses the question asked by Altrichter and Posch in their 1992 paper, 'are the understandings gained during a research process confronted with the perspective of other persons concerned?'.

The process of generating knowledge, of making claims in action research, or indeed in any form of research, brings up two key issues. One is the actual process of the sense-making. What can we say about its nature? The second is the issue of quality and rigour in research. How can we tell that the work was good work done well?

Making sense and claiming to know

For most of us, our everyday experiences and encounters with research have their genesis in a scientific paradigm, using a process known as deduction. Even research that is conducted in a social science environment is more often than not based on deductive processes. If we consider drug research, for example, normal practice is to conduct a set of randomised control trials and, on the basis of how the general or majority population responds to the treatment, generate a theory, test it and from this predict how an individual might respond. Thus, the epistemological direction is from the general to the specific. On the basis of the behaviour, description, responses of a large population, we predict behaviours, descriptions or responses of the individual. It is a powerful and efficacious technique when used appropriately. Given the complexity of the human condition, an approach such as this allows effective planning, managed commercial risk-taking, drug development and administration, and so forth, in the knowledge that the probability of an appropriate response or behaviour is high enough to counterbalance any exceptions. Thus, we see figures such as '93 per cent of respondents noticed a reduction in wrinkles after using product X', '9 out of 10 men said they reduced the rate of hair loss or even re-grew their hair with product Y' and other such majority-based claims. The fact that we buy such products is testament to our close connection to the deductive process. The reader sees such an advertisement, and immediately translates the general into the specific, and decides that it is a fairly safe bet that the product will work in the desired way for them.

For most people, much of the time, this approach works; as it should. It is, after all, based on a 'most people, much of the time' philosophy. However, for the few people for whom the product does not work, or produces in them unpleasant side-effects, the 'most people, much of the time' explanation can seem meaningless. What does it matter that most people suffered no ill effects if you are the one that did? As human beings, we exist in that paradoxical place where the power of the general can be comforting, yet can make us feel more isolated when we are not part of that 'general'. Teachers in classrooms can find themselves in this type of dilemma when they realise that a particular approach to behaviour management, for example, has not been effective in their classroom, despite it having been promoted as almost universally successful. Does its lack of success in their classroom say something about the inadequacy of the approach itself, or something uncomfortable about them as teachers? It is for reasons such as this that many teachers come to undertake action research as a process which recognises the specificity and particularities of their context and issues.

Generalisation

Action research is a process where we start with the specific, and through an exploration and analysis of it, begin to theorise about our own practice. While it does not seek to fully generalise from the specific (although Mejía (2010) argues that at every stage in the action research process, generalisation is taking place, and that the description of knowledge construction extends beyond the inductive and deductive processes), it does seek to produce understanding which can be shared, related and interrogated. Its approach bears more relationship to inductive processes, whose epistemological direction is from the specific to the general. Green (1999), in making the point that action research is always concerned with the particular, goes on to suggest that 'Its generalisations come from understandings about the way a very particular context can be recognised and explored and about the nature of the professional judgements made in response to those explorations' (Green, 1999: 106). This describes what has variously been called 'the philosophy of argument', 'informal logic', or more familiarly to educationalists, 'critical thinking'. These equivalences are disputed in some quarters, but for the purposes of this text, it is helpful to stick with the term 'critical thinking', so that we can relate the more inductive process of sense-making in action research to a concept we are familiar with in our practice.

The action researcher is first concerned, to paraphrase Popper (1972), with getting better acquainted with the problem. From the data generated, from reflection and analysis, and exploration in relation to literature and theoretical perspectives, the practitioner moves in an inductive manner through description and analysis into sense-making and knowledge claims.

Consider then how Susan could become better acquainted with her problem so that she can start to make warrantable and defensible claims about her practice. We have already alluded to the potential for her to have generated a further data set during the reconnaissance period through using her pupils as a validation set. Teachers can find this democratising aspect of action research conceptually and pragmatically difficult, as it begins to define a new set of classroom relationships. An alternative approach for Susan might have been follow-up interviews or focus groups with her pupils in which she could have used the two open-ended questionnaire items as prompts for the interview questions. The data from this process could then have been compared and contrasted with that from the questionnaires in a process known as triangulation. As Robson (2002: 370) states: 'One important benefit of multiple methods is in the reduction of inappropriate certainty. Using a single method and finding a pretty clear-cut result may delude investigators into thinking that they have found the "right" answer'. This is even more so in Susan's case where she has nothing against which to check her own analysis of that single set of findings.

Claiming to know

Claiming to know something is both a challenging and a challengeable position. At the simplest level, when you say you 'know' something, you need to be able to say how you know, and when challenged, show that your way of knowing is defensible. A valid evidence-base to back your knowledge claim is the normal defence presented. In other words, data has been collected, collated and analysed in a way that transforms it into evidence for the claim you are making.

However, knowledge itself is a complex and sometimes contested word, and one whose history reveals changes in meaning and use. Let us first of all consider two terms in philosophy used to explain the means by which we know something. The knowledge that we have regardless of our experiences, is identified as *a priori*. Often described as a process based on pure thought or reason, we reflect on the actual content of what has been said in order to establish its legitimacy. For example, if I tell you that my father is taller than me, and that I am taller than my sister, you can conclude, by applying reasoning and logic, that my father is taller than my sister. You do not have to have any experience of any one of us in order to know that this is the case. The justification for *a priori* knowledge therefore must be predicated on the person having a valid reason to believe that it is so. Truthfulness is perhaps one such reason. In order to *know* that my father is taller than my sister, you must be able to believe the information I have given you in the first two statements.

This, of course, leads to questions of where logical validity does not result in truthful outcomes. For instance, I could give you an often used example in the teaching of logic and say, 'All mammals are four-footed animals. All people are mammals; therefore, all people are four-footed animals.' Our closing statement here is logically valid, but untrue. If one or more of the premises of a logical argument is false, then the conclusion will also be false. The validity of an argument should therefore be distinguished from the truth of the conclusion, bringing us to the seemingly paradoxical notion of 'valid-but-untrue'.

The knowledge that we derive from, or construct on the basis of our experience is *a posteriori*. You know, for example, that the price of petrol has increased at a greater rate than your earnings, because you have experienced it. It is, in essence, an empiricist view of knowing. A simplistic view of this is that empirical knowledge is certain knowledge. Things, and their attributes, are fixed entities, and their behaviour predictable. The logic with which knowledge was constructed from empirical evidence was a logic of certainty, often thought of as a form of mathematical Boolean logic, predicated on clear causal relationships and defined stable states and boundaries. However, evidence from the field of science and mathematics at the start of the twentieth century seemed to indicate that probability rather than certainty was the essence of understanding. The understanding of the atom, for example, had until then been of a billiard ball-like structure, composed of a tiny nucleus, surrounded by orbiting electrons. New experimental evidence yielding new theories such as quantum theory described an atom, which had few, if any, certain attributes. The position of its electrons was described as probability waves, rather than as defined locations. Its behaviour was determined by the mathematics of probability. The face of science and mathematics was changed forever.

You may ask why all this is important in a book about action research in education. First, when we make claims to knowing I believe it is important that we understand some of the significance of this in both a philosophical as well as a pragmatic way. Secondly, and this is perhaps more important, I believe that there is still a form of logical positivism in us all when it comes to making knowledge claims. By this, I mean that we often seek to 'prove or verify' and, in doing so, suggest that proof is both an appropriate and a simple concept. We also have a desire for certainty, and a belief that the data we collect can provide that. The example above of the changing understanding of the structure of the atom is, I feel, a very powerful illustration that even in the field of pure science, understanding probability is more appropriate and useful than searching for certainty. The resonances of this with the new logic of probability, known as fuzzy logic, can be seen in Bassey's work on fuzzy generalisations (2001: 5), where he discusses the concept that certain actions in certain circumstances *may* have certain results. Discussing the possible corollary of this where the actions may not have certain results, he suggests that a way to overcome the rather limited usefulness of such causality statements, is through what he calls a 'Best Estimate of Trustworthiness' in which appropriate levels of contextual information are given so that the reader may make educated estimates of the likelihood of particular results happening in their own context. In this way, the claim to knowing resides with the reader rather than the writer, with the latter taking responsibility for providing enough information to aid the reader in this.

Provisionality

Claims to knowledge are often provisional and tentative, subject to further scrutiny and interrogation. At the same time, however, they must be able to be substantiated. McNiff deals with this in a very accessible way, saying that when you make a knowledge claim, you also need 'other people critically to consider your claim and agree that you have good reason for making your claim. They might agree that you are justified in making your claim, and their agreement would be validation of your claim. Conversely, as participants in your research, they may feel that your claim is based on a somewhat biased analysis, and thus challenge you to return to its underpinning premises' (McNiff, 2002: unpaginated). Later in the text, she cites as a criterion for judging quality in research reports the question 'Do you show that you can hold yourself accountable for your claims to knowledge?' I think this is a key question throughout the various stages of an action research report, and one which challenges you to demonstrate the ways in which you have provided for that accountability. The 'validation' of your findings by critical friends, research participants and others will form part of that. So also will your reading and the other ways in which you have supported the development of your own thinking and analysis.

In summary, the making of warrantable knowledge claims depends on the security of the evidence you collect (which is dependent on an appropriate and rigorous project design), the consideration of alternative interpretations, and the degree to which you have subjected your thinking to challenge and illumination. Making knowledge claims is clearly an activity predicated on having undertaken research of good quality.

Using the literature

This chapter would be incomplete without discussion of the place of 'the literature' in this process. Although Chapter 5 has discussed the way in which literature relates to the action research process, it is germane at this point to briefly explore just how it contributes to sense-making. Whatever model of action research is used, the end process is still that the researcher hopes to extract some key units of meaning from the data analysis. The normal critical and reflective thinking processes help make sense of these. Additionally, though, further insight can be gleaned through consulting relevant literature. While there is discussion and debate among action research aficionados about the need or desirability of conducting a preliminary literature review on commencing the project, there is no conflict of opinion in relation to literature at the analysis stage. In order to strengthen the claim to knowledge, it is important that the researcher demonstrates familiarity with the field.

Vygotsky agrees with me

This does not mean simply finding a perspective in the literature that seems to lend support for your perspective or analysis. Too often, the temptation to find one text that presents a similar analysis to the one at which you have arrived, is taken as validation of that analysis. Further, there is a tendency to report such congruence in rather alarming tones similar to: 'Vygotsky agrees with me in that the majority of my pupils learn better when I provide opportunities for collaborative dialogue.' Given that Vygotsky (1896–1934) has never been in any of my students' classrooms, let alone agreed with that student's analysis, it is a reminder to take care with both the single perspective and, more importantly in this case, the sentence structure used to discuss it.

A range of perspectives

It is important, therefore, to subject your findings to scrutiny in the light of the range of perspectives that you will find in the literature. It means being willing and able to challenge your own interpretations as a possible demonstration of bias. Most importantly, it means that, having done these things, you are able to robustly defend your analysis. This not only adds to the credibility of the work, but transforms it into scholarship, which connects with the work of others, and hence is enhanced in terms of its relevance outside its own specific context.

Summary

This chapter has outlined some ways in which we turn data into evidence. While this starts off as a somewhat 'mechanical' process, it can be seen that it is a process which brings us into conversation with concepts of the nature of knowledge and claims to know, and with notions of academic integrity and scholarship, and helps us understand how individual action research projects relate to, inform and are informed by the wider practice and research communities.

Further reading

Mertler, C. (2009) *Action Research: Teachers as Researchers in the Classroom*. Thousand Oaks, CA: Sage.

Chapter 6 of this text provides a clear insight into the processes involved in data management and analysis, interspersed with many examples and activities designed to build skill and proficiency. If you will be dealing with a significant amount of quantitative data and want to know more about the use of computer software in this, then you will find the chapter particularly useful.

Thomas, G. (2009) *How to do your Research Project*. London: Sage

Although not an action research book, this book deals with many matters which are common to practitioner research. Chapter 9 is particularly useful in terms of the ways in which data analysis leads to what he calls 'drawing out theory'. Some well illustrated examples of this process make the concept highly accessible to the reader.

Further online resources can be found at:
www.sagepub.co.uk/beraseries.sp

CHAPTER 7

WRITING UP AN ACTION RESEARCH PROJECT

The 'doing' of action research is often easier than the 'telling' of it. Because of the complexity, lack of predictability in practice situations and, above all, because of the centrality of the personal voice in it, many teachers struggle to find a way of presenting their work which maintains the integrity and authenticity of their actions and thoughts, while at the same time has an appropriate academic tone for the purposes of postgraduate assessment. For many master's students seeking advice from their tutors at this stage in their work, the first question they ask is 'Can I write this in the first person?' This is an important question.

In all writing, it is important to consider *purpose*, *audience* and *voice* before starting the work. At the risk of sounding somewhat patronising I would like to spend a little time on this before moving on. From my own perspective, I find that questions in relation to these three key factors come right at the start of any writing I do, and that 'purpose' and 'audience' are often related. I need to clarify what I want to convey, and to whom. Having done that, I find that the decision about voice is often one that almost makes itself. If I am writing up a report of an action research study, then I may, for example, want to write it for sharing with colleagues and peers in a way that is relatively academic, but very strongly focused on the narrative of the project and its significant findings or outcomes. If, on the other hand, I decide to write the account for possible publication in an academic journal, I may decide to reduce the narrative, and emphasise the section on methodology or discussion of findings in order to produce a more conceptually engaged piece of writing. Depending on the choice of academic journal, I may also change the voice. For the most part, accounts of action research are most likely to be found in journals that welcome first-person writing and value personal reflective writing. In other words, the report will deal with both the process *and* the outcomes of undertaking action research. On the other hand, outcomes from action research projects may be written up from a more theoretical perspective, with a focus on relating findings to key constructs in the field. It will be very much product orientated and the personal reflective voice may be neither needed nor, indeed, welcome. Deciding where to target the work will immediately identify the purpose and audience, and in doing so will strongly suggest the appropriate voice.

When writing accounts of practice-based action research and presenting them as academic assessment tasks on postgraduate programmes, the articulation of learning outcomes, or other module requirements, will normally give a fairly strong indicator of the nature of the work to be undertaken, the purpose of it and the implied voice. Phrases such as 'critically reflect on your role as . . .', 'critically evaluate and reflect on an aspect of your leadership practice . . .' and 'demonstrate a critically reflective awareness of your professional learning and development' indicate the need for a personal response to practice, and hence are suggestive of a personal voice in the writing of that response. Writers such as Moon (2006) and Ghaye and Ghaye (1998) all highlight the affective or emotional aspect of reflecting on learning. Such pointers, therefore, are suggestive of a highly personalised piece of writing and not only position the author centrally, but also suggest a first-person narrative response. Indeed, if we consider action research as living theory, or at least akin to it, then it would seem incongruent to write reports in anything other than the first person.

Who are you?

Ahmed has been undertaking a piece of action research in his school in relation to supporting young disaffected pupils. He is leader of year 9, and in that capacity has worked with the year 9 tutors and a group of pupils from the year. He is also form tutor to a group of year 9 pupils and, in addition, teaches French to a class group. Over the period of a term, he has implemented a number of changes based on the findings from his study, and is now at the stage of writing up the account for his assessed piece of work. He feels that he needs to adopt a fairly formal approach to his writing in order to 'make it more academic', and opts to write in the third person. He asks his tutor to look at a draft of the work in progress, as he is finding the writing process rather challenging.

The tutor finds the draft rather difficult to read and, in particular, is confused by the characters in the story. She identifies a number of phrases and sentences as particularly confusing for her, as follows:

- The researcher himself notes that . . .
- The class teacher found that when a new approach to French homework had been negotiated, the children seemed more inclined to complete it.
- The year leader realised the importance of all tutors singing from the same hymn sheet.

Her comment to Ahmed was 'Who are these people, and what is their relationship to you? Where is your voice in this project?' It had taken the tutor some time during her reading to realise that the researcher, the class teacher and the year leader were one and the same person. She needed to show Ahmed how confusing it was for a reader to come across multiple articulations of the same person.

Commentary

Like many people new to action research, the notion of writing up an academic piece in the first person is as new to them as some of the concepts they have encountered along the way. The concept of academic quality can seem so inextricably linked to the concept of objectivity that first-person accounts seem to represent everything that a research report should not be. The traditional research report normally avoids the first-person voice and, in doing so, seems to convey a degree of objectivity and academic authority to the reader. For many teachers and other practitioners, this perceived sense of authority is particularly significant in influencing them to write in the third person. Feeling that their project is small scale and 'amateur', they can feel that writing in the third person lends a sense of authority and credibility. For those who have never written in the first person before, or who have a subject discipline where third-person writing was required, there can almost be a sense of disbelief that first-person writing can really be either appropriate or academically acceptable. It is, perhaps, a somewhat overlooked part of the postgraduate tutor's role to expose the students to a range of writing styles, which includes academically acceptable first-person writing. When students read research reports in their own areas of interest, the reports they read have often been written in the third person, passive voice, and any part written in the first voice positioned as an illustrative case study report. This can have the effect of suggesting that the 'story' is somehow lesser than the rest of the report and, while helpful for the reader, does not carry any academic weight or credibility of its own.

Reflection

Why do you think Ahmed might have elected to write in a third person voice? What might be the perceived advantages of doing so? What might be the disadvantages? How do you think you would advise him?

Tell it like it is

My own written reflections on early action research projects and their articulation in written assignments reveal a real struggle to find my voice. As an avid reader, I was perhaps suffering from having read too much. I spent many hours in the university library reading dissertations from previous cohorts of students on my programme and, with each one, feeling more and more despondent. The overwhelming feeling was 'I couldn't write like that', and in saying that, I was also saying 'I couldn't write as well as that'. This became particularly problematic for me as I started writing up my final dissertation, where the size of the task (in those days, it was a 20,000-word piece) seemed to exacerbate my sense of inadequacy. Despite having written assignments for the earlier part of the course, which had been reports of action research projects, I was still struggling both philosophically and linguistically with action research. Somehow I seemed to be able to embrace it at a relatively superficial level (to paraphrase Hammersley (2006), as a technique rather than as a philosophy) but, on having the longer period of time and the scope to read and reflect more widely during the final dissertation stage, I began to see the gaps in my knowledge and understanding. This was particularly evident when I tried to structure and write up the larger final year project. I found a need to write up a clean linear account, but did not know how to do that for a process that was non-linear, and indeed messy. I wanted to present something that was authentic and personal, but found that accounts I was reading in books and journals seemed to be tidy and betray none of the more authentic 'mess' that I was experiencing. Advice from my supervisor to 'tell it like it is' was initially interpreted by me as a suggestion that I write it as an almost Joycean stream of consciousness. While the suggested authenticity of this 'tell it like it is' appealed to me, the thought of anyone having to read such an unstructured diatribe filled me with horror. On the other hand, I also remember being very disengaged by some of the action reports which I read. Their clear and lucid structure, the way in which everything came across as not in the least problematic, suggested to me that there was something inauthentic and sanitised about them. Telling it as it was, in a way that remained readable, was a major challenge in my dissertation, and remains a challenge when I write anything that is as multi-stranded as an action research report.

Reflection

Think about your own experiences of reading and writing action research. Where have you seen most action research reports or accounts? Do you think they 'tell it like it is'? In this context, what do you think 'tell it like it is' suggests?

Commentary

In the years since this experience, I have come to understand the phrase 'tell it like it is' in a number of different ways. At one level it is a call for authenticity, in that the account should be true to the data. Inexperienced action researchers often feel reluctant to give their own data credibility. Throughout the book, and in Chapter 6 in particular, we see the difficulties of working in a discourse that dominates, but differs from, that of action research. This is one reason why accounts of practice tend at times to draw less on data from that practice than they should. The seduction of a dominant discourse, or some respected author's suggested causes for underachievement, for example, may mean that their own accounts are not true to their practice. Analyses are informed more by external influences than the data themselves, which can lead to misinterpretation. Thus, 'telling it like it is' is a call for an acknowledgement and respect for the data generated in the project.

Two other interpretations of this phrase also seem important to me. First, I believe that telling it like it is is a directive to the writer, bringing with it the question 'What is it like, for you?' Thus, it also brings with it the challenge of articulating the issues and problems involved in the project, the complexities of it, the unexpectedness of it, and the richness of it. In other words, it relates to the process of action research, as well as the outcomes.

Secondly, I have observed from my own early experiences in writing, and from many years of supporting students in their writing, that it is not at all uncommon to find a student writing in a somewhat awkward, constructed voice. The desire to make the work seem academic can make people try to emulate other writing styles, with the result that accounts of their own practice seems somehow not to be in their own voice. This is a challenging issue for student and tutor alike, and the advice to read more is often appropriate in order that the student or novice may be exposed to good first-person writing. It is important, however, to help students to read this as 'someone else's voice', looking for some of the strategies and devices which authors have used to make the work both engaging and authentic. Finding your own voice, your own writing style, is something that comes with practice in both reading and writing. In my own case, it took quite some time before I developed the confidence to write it 'my way' while still being sensitive to, and informed by, reading other ways.

In addition to action research reports requiring a truthful representation and analysis of the data, and authenticity in voice and style, we need to remember that they are also forms of narrative, or story. They tell of our journey through change and development, our interpersonal encounters along the way, and our internal grappling with the complexity of both theory and practice.

The importance of the story

The role of narrative in action research has been recognised by authors such as Bold (2012) and Johnson (2008) who suggests that in the report of any project, entering 'teaching mode' enables the necessary narrative of the project to be told. Assuming that the reader knows nothing ensures both clarity and simplicity in the narrative. Writing the story is also a mechanism whereby we can write one layer of a report in a way that provides a supporting structure for the rest. As such, it represents a device through which a more analytic narrative may emerge. It is in the telling of a story that its main points may become obvious. Its structuring and telling is a heuristic device, enabling both the writer and the reader to ask more questions and explore more concepts. This, of course, can result in different questions and concepts on revisiting the account. In our day-to-day lives, we are all familiar with the notion of a story changing in the telling, or of that moment when a different interpretation is suddenly made manifest, even though the story has been told or heard on numerous occasions. We tend to understand our pathway through our lives as a meaning-making process, continuously questioning and responding to the context in which we find ourselves. Reflecting on past events, for example, often brings new insights or understandings, as we bring different levels of experience or maturity to them. Clough (2002) uses this approach in his research, employing what he calls a 'storying methodology', recognising that the telling of the story is, in itself, a construction of its meaning. Researchers who employ such a narrative approach to their research acknowledge that not only is knowledge constructed in its communication, but that there is no one single 'truth' in its articulation.

While a discussion of 'truth/truths' is conceptually large, and beyond the scope of this book, it is an issue worth remembering as you write the narrative of your action research project. How, for example, do you ensure that your report does not demonstrate a misuse of what Adams (2008) calls 'narrative privilege'? How do you attempt to ensure that a story full of complex and changing relationships and events is not simply yours? Discussions in Chapter 6 in relation to multiple perspectives and the use of critical friends and validation sets remind us of some ways in which this may be ameliorated. As a writer of such accounts, the responsibility is yours to ensure their lack of bias.

Building the story

Bold (2012: 153) talks of 'layered stories' in which narratives from different perspectives on the same event are used to construct a final narrative which is more representative of the 'reality of the learning situation, thus suggesting that the content is reliable and trustworthy'. This form of triangulation is often used in constructing and interrogating the evidence base in an action research project. I also like to use the term 'layered stories' to illustrate the process of writing up or constructing an action research report. Starting from the simple narrative of what happened when, where and with whom, I encourage students to build layers onto this, in much the same way as Jenny Moon (2006) encourages the building up of personal reflection accounts. Adapting from the work of the philosopher Gilbert Ryle, Geertz (1973) uses the term 'thick description' to mean a highly contextualised description that can allow outside readers access to as much of a situation as possible. This should be the first layer of writing, in that it allows both the writer and reader to review and reflect on the context and basic story of the project. In my experience, many students try to move straight to analytic writing without doing this, and assume a reader's familiarity that does not exist. In addition though, and I believe this to be equally if not more important, the act of carefully constructing the initial thick description provides a reflective space and is an analytic as well as a narrative device. In many ways, I feel that academics have almost encouraged their master's-level students to treat this phase with less worth than it needs by using phrases in feedback such as 'your work is too descriptive, and lacks critical reflection or analysis', 'you need to move beyond the descriptive to a more analytic approach in your writing', and so forth. It is possible that in emphasising the need for critical reflection and analysis for work at this level, we appear to devalue, or at least undervalue, the importance of description, and of the story. Yet, even at the most superficial level, we cannot, as readers, understand the analysis if we do not know to what it refers. Knowledge of the order in which a number of events happened may be crucial in our understanding of responses to them. The skilful layering of a story allows both the building of thick description, helping the reader to more fully understand what happened, where, with whom, and why, while at the same time providing a structure for the development of ongoing reflection and sense-making. For this reason, I often encourage students to 'write it all down' at the start, to bring their work into a basic story, so that, with that story as an underlying skeleton, layers of meaning can be added through personal reflection, through data analysis, through conversations with the literature, and so forth. It may be that in later edits, some of the material may have to be removed, but it is only at this later stage that such a decision can be made.

'Difficult' stories

One of the problems facing anyone researching their own practice is the possibility of difficult or sensitive data emerging. While it may seem imperative that the data is retained, its presentation in a report may be problematic for the writer. How, for example, can it be written in a non-judgemental way? How can it be shared without causing hurt or upset? Should it be shared? How can the report be considered to have integrity if it is not included? Questions such as these can, and indeed should, trouble researchers at all stages in their career. For the novice action researcher, however, the realisation that their research project has the potential to uncover sensitive issues, and expose what could be seen as weaknesses in practice, can be quite shocking.

In my opinion, the questions provoked fall into two broad categories. In the first instance, there is an issue of whether or not the data *should* be included, and with that question come discussions around ethics, integrity, and professional and personal relationships. The second type of question relates more to the *mechanism* by which such sensitive information, if deemed necessary, may be included.

Reflection

Think back on something that has happened recently in your workplace. It may be a restructuring in relation to management, some changes in roles and responsibilities, a change in teaching, or learning and assessment policies, for example. If you had been doing some research in the area, do you think you would have uncovered some sensitive situations? Would you have found any of it difficult to share in a more public forum? How do you think you might cope with a situation like this?

Should difficult stories be told?

First, it is imperative that those undertaking research in their own workplace, and those supervising such research, are sensitive to matters of professional protocols and relationships. In my experience, it is not unusual to find a relatively inexperienced, but ambitious, teacher undertaking professional development programmes in relation to their own leadership aspirations. While not wishing to make gross generalisations or simplifications, I would say that neither is it unusual to find something of an 'I would do things better if I was the team leader' attitude in these aspiring leaders. It is not surprising that these traits should be present in aspiring leaders, but without the tempering of experience, they can cause problems for school-based researchers. Having identified what can be seen as evidence of bad decision-making or poor leadership, for example, there is a temptation in some quarters to expose it in the report. On occasion, I have supervised students where the production of such data has been through biased collection methods or sources, and no attempt has been made to find an alternative view. On almost every occasion where I have come across situations like this, the person or people concerned have not had a chance to see or respond to the analysis produced. In some cases, they were unaware that data had been collected about them. Such practices lack both academic and ethical integrity, and my advice to students is always to consider both matters strongly in relation to the decision they make about including the material. Without considerations of alternative perspectives on the situation in question, the data produced, and hence its analysis, must be seen as incomplete and lacking in academic integrity. The alternative perspectives may indeed reveal reasons why a certain decision, although seemingly a poor one, was in fact the most appropriate within a particular context or set of constraints. To report it as a poor or weak decision is both factually incorrect and unfair to those concerned.

This brings us to the matter of ethical integrity. It cannot be seen as an ethically defensible stance to produce and publish materials which, in being incorrect, portray someone in a bad light, or in a way that is damaging both personally and professionally for them. Even paying only scant attention to ethics codes of practice (such as those produced by the British Educational Research Association or other professional and academic bodies) will suggest that the undertaking and reporting of research should not cause harm. While taking into account that, on the whole, reports produced by teachers on postgraduate education programmes have a rather limited readership, there is no guarantee that there will not be some negative fallout from the writing of such a report. In a world of ever-increasing connection and connectivity, it is difficult to predict the effects our actions may have, or the hurt that may be caused by such a report.

We can see, then, that the question as to whether or not difficult stories should be told does not have an easy answer. It is a question, however, that each practitioner-researcher must consider carefully. Decisions made become their own professional responsibility and must therefore be carefully thought through so that the decision reached can be justified and satisfy personal values and beliefs. For novice researchers, the support of a tutor at this time can be really helpful.

How should difficult stories be told?

The second type of question relates to the ways in which sensitive information can be included, for it must be acknowledged that almost all research will uncover something sensitive. In some cases, the careful positioning of such information, the construction of a non-judgemental narrative around it, and the clear demonstration of alternative perspectives can be skilfully done so that the finished product is neither offensive, nor potentially harmful. Some writers adopt particular strategies for doing this in a way where the issues which arise can be presented and discussed, but in a somewhat less personal way. Bold (2012) discusses the way in which 'fictionalised narrative', or as she prefers to call it 'representative construction', can be used effectively to pull together diverse data in a framework which is 'readable and meaningful' (Bold, 2012: 146). She describes this as a process of reconceptualising, and a means by which a writer can deal with conflict situations, and as a possible (though carefully considered) response to issues of confidentiality and anonymity. Evans (1997) uses the term 'storying' to describe the methodology by which she both tells and attempts to understand a difficult situation in her action research project. In constructing what could be seen as a rather allegorical tale, she provides a framework for the telling of, and the thinking about, the challenges she was facing in her work with others in her school.

People may develop a range of ways of telling difficult stories, and in most cases of action research, it is reasonable to assume that the project will have the potential to generate some sensitive data. While the final decision about how to report it may to an extent be dependent on the data, it is something that does need to be considered early in the study. The construction of a storying approach, such as that of Evans (1997), requires early planning, and, as Evans alludes to, it is as much a decision of methodology as it is of reporting. For all practice-based research that is undertaken as part of professional development programmes, there is another reason why practitioners need to think about this right at the start. The use of storying reports or constructed narratives may not find favour in some quarters, so conversations around these approaches need to be undertaken early, and with the support of a tutor.

The Council of European Social Science Data Archives (CESSDA) provides some practical guidelines on their website (http://www.cessda.org). The eight-point list contains reminders to anonymise, to take care with potential identifiers (in a school context, describing teacher X as a newly qualified teacher in the science department is probably just as clear a pointer to the teacher's identity as their name is) and so forth. However, techniques such as aggregation of characteristics, or what they refer to as 'Collapsing and/or combining variables – merging the concepts embodied in two or more variables by creating a new summary variable' are not so often discussed in research texts. Their use, however, allows some potential for reducing the possibility of unnecessary participant identification. It is also worth pointing out that school-based research reports may be published on websites, or held (in the case of MA dissertations) in a university library, and so perhaps the most important consideration in writing up reports is whether or not you, as author of the report, are happy for it to be read by your participants.

Protection of raw data

For the researcher, discussions of difficult stories and other matters of sensitivity highlight the need to consider matters of security in relation to data storage. Throughout the process, the researcher will be in possession of a quantity of raw data, possibly sensitive in nature, and always given on the understanding that the researcher will maintain confidentiality. Some years ago the use of secure locked cupboards was necessary, but as the bulk of data is now stored (or even captured) electronically, the use of password-protected data storage media is a simple but practical step that can be taken.

A story has a start, middle and end

When we look at attempts to depict the action research process visually, we see cyclic and spiral representations, immediately suggestive of a process that is certainly not linear, and in some cases may not even have a very clearly identified starting point. While it is certainly the case that the researcher will have had to start somewhere, the explanation of that starting point will often take us back in time, allowing us to understand the context in which the project is happening. The researcher often provides some personally reflective narrative, explaining their personal as well as professional interest in the project, and outlining something of their own beliefs and values. This personal reflection can run as a thread through the whole project. While this is all well within the spirit of action research, and will almost certainly act as a personal compass throughout the project, its interwoven nature can make writing the report difficult. Likewise, an ongoing and conversational relationship between data and literature can cause difficulties in report writing. In many cases, university support materials for students engaging on a research project relate more to theory-testing than theory-generating approaches, emulating to some extent that of a traditional dissertation, with five chapters as follows:

1 Introductory chapter, setting the scene and context, articulating the research question, and justifying the importance of the topic
2 The literature review, demonstrating familiarity with what is already written and relating it to the research focus in question
3 The methodology chapter, outlining the methodological framework which will be used for the study, and within it, the methods by which data will be collected and analysed
4 The presentation and analysis of research findings
5 The concluding chapter incorporating a discussion of the findings, conclusions and recommendations (for practice), and in practitioner research, some reflections on the project.

The preceding section of this chapter touches on issues relating to writing the 'messiness' of action research, and the importance of articulating this mess. From Schön talking about the 'swampy lowlands' in 1983 through to the work of Mellor (2001) and Cook (1998, 2009), the importance of this 'mess' as a place where thinking changes, interpretations are challenged and meaning is made, is stressed. These authors would argue that this mess brings value and rigour. Cook suggests that it is 'vital to research that seeks to engage in contesting knowledge leading to changes in practice' (Cook, 2009: 285).

In many cases, acknowledgement and discussion of this mess finds its way into 'methodology' sections, explaining how changes in a planned approach may be necessary in response to feedback from cycles of action research. It may also be located in a 'discussion' or 'reflection' section, where the writer seeks to articulate some of the challenges and difficulties that have been encountered in their project. In suggesting that he may 'wish to draw on a range of techniques and ideas in dealing with the messy reality of my research practice' (2001: 478), Mellor identifies the ways in which action research not only must cope with the unexpected, but must also be similarly constituted in and of itself. Davies's (2007) paper, 'Rethinking the architecture: an action researcher's resolution to writing and presenting their thesis' gives an idea of how one practitioner attempted to do this.

In discussing the difficulties she had in writing up her own action research report, Davies explains how she used Elliott's (1994) criteria to help her first conceptualise what she needed to do. Drawing on his work, she does this by articulating what she wanted her report to do, suggesting that it should:

- provide a narrative account of the change process as it unfolds from a variety of perspectives: researcher, teachers, parents. This should tell a story in non-technical language and give the reader a sense of what it was like to be involved;
- portray the change process in context, highlighting those aspects which illuminate the experience of those involved;
- focus on problematic aspects of the change process;
- reflect upon these problematic aspects from different angles or points of view;
- reveal how understanding of the situation and the problems and issues evolved, in the light of new evidence;
- describe the curriculum and pedagogical strategies generated during the course of developing understanding of the situation;
- assess the consequences of curriculum and pedagogical strategies, both intended and unintended, for the quality of the change process; and
- describe, justify and critique the methods and procedures used to gather and analyse data. (Davies, 2007: 194)

Davies uses this guidance to help produce her report in which she rethinks the architecture of a thesis, and in doing so provides a meaningful and rich insight into the ways in which her deeply reflective and reflexive process helped her develop understanding of her practice. She describes this as a process of '"weaving back and forth" between literature review, data analysis and interpretation, by placing multiple literature reviews throughout the thesis' (Davies, 2007: 194), with each chapter providing 'a mix of narrative, critical commentary, literature review, data analysis and interpretation' (ibid).

This sophisticated revision of the traditional thesis structure is challenging for both the writer and the reader. On presenting her thesis for examination, Davies reports the difficulty one examiner had with her work, and his comments in relation to the lack of a traditional literature review to inform the substantive element of her study. For a confident PhD student, this was challenging. For a first-time action researcher, this type of challenge is likely to feel insurmountable. Further, there is an opportunity at a PhD viva to discuss and defend the work. In taught postgraduate programmes, this is not usually the case. As a tutor on such programmes I am conscious that students should not be placed in vulnerable positions in relation to the assessment of their work, but also conscious that work of this type needs to be presented in a way that is an authentic representation of their engagement with the research.

Reflection

Think about your own study and consider the ways in which you might first of all 'tell its story' to a colleague or friend. Contemplate the possible structure of what you would say, the (mental) headings you might use to help you talk it through, and the things that you would actually say. You might find it useful at this point to jot down possible headings and bullet points.

Now reflect on the standard research report headings:

1 Context, introduction and research question
2 Literature review
3 Methodology and project design
4 Findings and analysis
5 Discussion, conclusion and recommendations.

How closely does this list 'fit' with what you have just done? How might you design your own outline structure if you had total freedom to do so?

The mode of presentation of action research reports is a rather under-discussed area in much contemporary literature. McMahon and Jefford describe the way in which an MA action research dissertation was failed at final examination, presenting the 'narrative of this event . . . to explore the central dilemma of assessing action-research reports inside academic programmes; namely, the competing needs of the action-researcher to follow the investigation wherever it leads and the need for the student to meet pre-set criteria for assessment' (McMahon and Jefford, 2009: 359).

Their paper is both interesting and important in that, not only does the narrative present an insight into the assessment process in a way that is much more transparent than the norm, but it raises real questions about the possibility of pre-specifying criteria against which to assess quality. McMahon (the tutor in question) discusses the way in which he feels that, in slavishly adhering to a pre-specified set of assessment criteria, he had turned 'action research into a technology, an oppressive instrument which can potentially distort other people's creative practice' (McNiff, 2002: 52) Drawing on the work of Elliott (2007), he revisits his concept of 'quality' in action research, and comes to a position where he agrees that criteria should neither be universal nor universalising, but must be adaptable to context. Suggesting that, 'regardless of type, action research should be judged by the three principles of theoretical and method-ological robustness, value-for-use and the potential to enable beneficial change; but within these generalities, more context-specific criteria can be applied to each class' (McMahon and Jefford, 2009: 361), he begins to reconceptualise his own concept of valid and legitimate action research and the ways in which academic criteria could assess it as such.

While the previous discussion focuses on quality, rather than mode of presentation, it raises a corresponding question about mode of presentation, or 'writing up'. The work of Cook in this regard (1998, 2009) is important in that it gives voice to the fact that, not only is action research a necessarily messy process, but also that the messiness needs to be articulated. Starting from a 'because it is there' (Cook, 2009: 279) justification, she goes on to explore the way in which its articulation is helpful for other researchers, emphasising that unless it is made clear, its role and purpose, and indeed its very existence in research, go unacknowledged.

This mess is a thread that has run through previous chapters of the book. It is my experience that while students are skilfully guided and supported through the messiness of their projects, relatively few are given help to find ways of articulating it. McMahon is hardly unique in working within pre-specified assessment criteria. Likewise, the support and scaffolding for students at the actual writing stage tends to produce structures which are pre-specified, and often unsuited to an action research methodology. Cook's work tackles this head on, drawing analogies from the work of Cubist art which attempted to present mul-tiple viewpoints and perspectives in a piece of work. She goes on to say that 'The subjects of the painting were broken up, analysed, re-assem-bled and re-presented in a way that meant the viewer had to engage with the image in an active and enquiring manner'. (Cook, 2009: 280).

The paper provides a rich philosophical insight into ways of knowing and the generation of new ways of knowing and seeing. It suggests that the messy area 'provides the space for clarification of the already known (explicit knowledge) and what is nearly known (implicit or tacit knowledge)' (Cook, 2009: 282). Her belief is that it is only through entering these messy areas, through confronting the challenges within them, that people can contest knowledge and effect changes in practice. She concludes by exhorting all action researchers to clearly articulate this process, not as an aside, but as an integrated part of the action research report: 'If an indicator of our successful work as action researchers is the integration of the development of practice with the construction of research knowledge, then we must provide honest accounts of that process and incorporate mess as an integral part of a rigorous approach'. (Cook, 2009: 290).

Providing honest accounts

If we draw together the work of Elliott, McMahon and Jefford, and Cook, we arrive at a position where we could describe good action research (and by extension, good action research reports) as having the following (broad and contextualisable) characteristics:

- theoretical and methodological robustness,
- value for use
- the potential to enable beneficial change
- authentic representation of learning and changing.

Reflection

If you were writing guidelines for students to help them in the presentation of their action research reports, how might you ensure that any advice on structuring was helpful in producing work that might meet these criteria? What might that advice look like? What would be helpful for you?

In my own practice I have found a dilemma between challenging and supporting students. As tutor, I want to challenge. As assessor of their work, I want to know I have supported them effectively. As a former student I also remember the need to feel secure in what I was being asked to do. Perhaps it is slightly dodging the issue, perhaps it is simply realism, but whichever it is, I have found that providing students with a seemingly linear structure helps their confidence both in themselves as new researchers and reporters, and in me as their tutor. However, while presenting this in a seemingly linear framework, I do attempt to build in sufficient challenge, and acknowledgement of the difficulty of pre-specification. I tend to give my students a set of key areas that should be addressed within any report, and within each area, a subset of prompt questions or notes indicating some pointers that they probably should consider in their report. While I am presenting this set of prompts (see boxed text), I think it is important to stress that it is not a pro forma. It is not a prescription. Neither is it meant as a 'running order' of the report – although some choose to use it in this way. What it is, is a discussion framework that I use with my students as we talk through the structure of their report. What is missing from it, and forms a key part of the discussion process, is the fact that throughout the process there will be a thread of personal and professional reflection. The role of the self in action research is central, and as such integrates into, interrogates, and is interrogated by, each stage in the process.

While this discussion framework may be of some help to you as you prepare to write up your own work, I would suggest that its use would be much enhanced were you to use it with tutors or colleagues as a discussion prompt, using and adapting as best suits the needs of your own work and your own writing style.

Introduction to you and your project

- What is the project about and why is it important for you to undertake it?
- Will you be able to take action based on your findings?
- Remember that your reader needs to know about the context within which your project is taking place.
- What are the key issues you hope to address?

Your starting point, project methodology and design

- Clearly state your starting point, bearing in mind that it may not be fully defined at this stage.
- What questions will you ask (and of whom) in trying to find out? Remember to ensure that you have permission before you start.
- Explain why action research is an appropriate methodology, and explain whether (and how) you are following a particular model. What literature will you draw on to support the choice you have made?

(Continued)

(Continued)

- Discuss any limitations you feel there may be in your work, and how you hope to ameliorate them.
- Clearly explain how you are ensuring that your project adheres to a set of ethical guidelines.
- What quality criteria are you using in your study, and why?
- Clearly explain or describe the methods by which you will collect and analyse initial data.
- Explain how this analysis will fit into a cyclic action research project – remember that the reader should be able to follow clearly your project design.

Evidence presentation and analysis

- How do you present your data? Think carefully about how you can best make them accessible to a reader. (Use graphs and charts with care. Ensure that they present information clearly, are labelled accurately and use an appropriate scale). Remember that you will probably have a lot of text-based data, and need to consider how to give voice to your participants.
- What are the main themes that are emerging?
- How do they relate to your initial (or in later cycles, refined) research questions?

Data interpretation: multi-directional conversations

- Can you identify any patterns or interesting links between sets of data? Agreements and disagreements? Are there any unexpected findings or contradictions?
- What does the substantive literature have to say that might help you explain and make meaning?
- Can you develop an argument based on your analysis? Can you plan for action on the basis of this?
- What specific actions will/can you take, and for how long/how often? Remember to describe the implementation of your action plan so that the reader can understand exactly what you plan to do.

Implementing, monitoring and evaluating the action plan

- Have you let the reader know what the implementation 'looks like'?
- How will you monitor it? What data will help you evaluate its success or otherwise?

- When you review and evaluate it, can you explain any successes and failures? How does the literature help with this?

- Either review and refine your original research focus/question and undertake another cycle, *or* in a final cycle, review your own personal and professional learning.

Conclusion

- What are the implications of your study? What have you learned? How will it impact on future practice? Do you see any avenues for further research and exploration?

- How do you think others might benefit from your findings? Might they be in any way relatable to other contexts and situations?

- Can you evaluate the research process itself? Is there anything you would have approached differently? Have you discovered any new areas for further enquiry?

- What have you learned about yourself in doing this study?

Reflection

How useful do you find this discussion framework in the light of your own action research experiences? Does it allow you to report your research in a way that works for you? Does it give you the scope to report on, address and discuss the challenges you encountered? Does it structure your report in a way that meets your requirements as well as any requirements of your university programme?

Summary: a story has a beginning, a middle and an end – or has it?

The undertaking of an action research project is complex. Reporting it is possibly more so. During this chapter we have explored some of the issues involved in producing the report, and dealt with some of the dilemmas faced when trying to produce a 'tidy' report of an untidy process. Hopefully, you will have taken heart from hearing of similar experiences of other, more experienced, researchers.

Your project will have taken you through cycles of practice and cycles of thought. Although having a defined starting point, you will have felt the need to revisit aspects of the past in order to understand the context and genesis of your concern. There is no sense of 'middle' in the usual sense of the word, and the decision to stop is usually pragmatic (often based on the need to submit a report within a given time frame), but in stopping, you are not signalling that there is no work left to begin. The end is thus a place which heralds new directions and new beginnings, acting as a launchpad for fresh investigations.

What you will have seen is that your report will necessarily be multilayered. It will, of necessity, have certain key features, but they will be overlaid with layers of descriptive narrative, of personal reflection and of analytic narrative. Throughout the report, there will be evidence of multiple conversations at work; conversations between you and the data, conversations between different sets of data, between you and yourself (as you reflect back on events, or trouble your way through dilemmas), between data and literature, and, perhaps most importantly, conversations between you and professional colleagues and critical friends. If I had to give just one piece of advice in relation to the presentation of the report, it would be to try to make these conversations come alive in your writing. Sharing a project account in this way produces a rich authenticity, and a narrative integrity that both illustrates and enhances the action research process itself.

Further reading

Cook, T. (2009): 'The purpose of mess in action research: building rigour though a messy turn', *Educational Action Research*, 17(2): 277–91.

This paper, developing from and building on her 1998 paper, illustrates the relationship between mess and rigour, discussing their apparent lack of compatibility, and shows how their acknowledgement and interrogation are essential elements in action research accounts in that through doing so, the researcher illustrates to the reader the importance of the 'messy turn', where profound learning occurs.

McMahon, T. and Jefford, E. (2009): 'Assessing action-research projects within formal academic programmes: using Elliott's context-related criteria to resolve the rigour versus flexibility dilemma', *Educational Action Research*, 17(3): 359–71.

This paper, co-written by a tutor and student after an MA dissertation was failed, unpicks the concept of rigour, and the nature and structure of academic writing. It will be a helpful paper for students and tutors alike, challenging some of the assumptions that are often evident in academic frameworks, and it highlights alternative frameworks for presenting and assessing the highly contextualised reports of action research studies.

Additional online resources can be found at:
www.sagepub.co.uk/beraseries.sp

SECTION 3

SHARING ACTION RESEARCH

CHAPTER 8

CONCLUSION: SHARING AND PROMOTING ACTION RESEARCH

This final chapter returns to the initial focus on the nature of action research, the models and processes by which it is normally undertaken, and the purposes and values it encapsulates. It discusses ways in which action research moves from the particularities of situated practice to speak to a broader audience.

If you have read this book prior to undertaking an action research project, you may be forgiven for thinking that the process can be quite a challenge. If, on the other hand, you are already engaged in or have previously done some action research, I hope that you have found some resonance with your own experiences.

It should be clear that action research is driven by a desire to understand practice, to question and critique it, and to expose it to interrogation, all with an underpinning aim of improving that practice. It is predicated upon a commitment to reflective practice, the values of democracy, and the scholarship of practice. While its purpose is stated as the improvement of professional practice, there is often an associated, more enriching, profound and positive effect on people's professional lives.

Let us reflect then, in the light of the previous chapters, just what this thing called action research actually is. In this chapter I attempt to do two things. In the first instance, through the use of short extracts from teachers' own reflections on their action research projects, I hope to explain some of the benefits of undertaking this approach, and in this way justify just why it is so important that accounts of action research projects are shared. Secondly, I hope to explore a range of means by which such findings may be effectively shared.

Why we should share action research accounts

In years of supervising action research projects the thing that strikes me most is the very real and deep changes that people experience in both their own professional lives and practices, and the impact that action research has on their colleagues and in their settings. They almost universally talk of the ways in which they have exposed their assumptions and practice to critical questioning, how unanticipated insights have caused them to reconceptualise their relationships with pupils, and with colleagues, and how these processes have helped them articulate their own beliefs and values, and more fully live them in practice.

Another aspect of their reflections is worth noting also. Despite most of the teachers having significant experience and expertise in their field, they have found themselves to be as novices again, finding new ways of doing a job in which they had previously been considered proficient. It seems to me that to experience outcomes such as these, suggests a moral imperative to share them with others. The potential to change practice, to impact positively on yourself, your colleagues and your pupils is something too important to keep hidden.

In many action research reports, the final section often presents a more personalised type of reflection, outlining the personal and professional insights gained during the project. I now want to present extracts from a number of such reflections, reproduced exactly as they are in final dissertations. They raise a range of important issues in educational practice, with each illustrating aspects of renewed understanding of previous practice. These written words, the product of a one-year project that has caused much soul-searching, say more than I could in relation to their own lived experiences of having engaged in the process. With each extract, I will present a very short contextualisation and narrative.

Reflection 1

This was written by Judy, a teacher of almost 20 years' experience, talented in both pastoral and pedagogic matters. At the end of her year-long project, she took some time to reflect on the things that had made most difference to her in her own professional knowledge and practice. Despite feeling that she had a strong and well-founded relationship with pupils, she was to find that her project brought fresh and deeper understandings. Challenging her very concept of her own professional role, she found that her pupils' voices had become a central part of her practice, promoting more democratic and respectful processes in her classroom.

> The professional challenge for me has been to become more reflective about my practice, uncover truths and deal with them. Consequently this has required me to undertake a new approach to practice and move from a didactic approach to a more participatory student-centred approach, and develop a more democratic classroom. The action research has helped me investigate previously misunderstood and unexplored aspects of the teacher–pupil relationship which have affected the quality of those relations to make sure that 'learning is best promoted in a context of trust, respect and confidence' (Carnell and Lodge, 2002: 23).

Reflection 2

Roberta had undertaken a rather challenging project in relation to children's play, and was surprised to find that she knew much less than she had thought about the nature, structure and support mechanisms involved. Faced with the particular challenge of a class group who had responded differently to any other in her experience, she found that as she canvassed the voices of these small children, she developed a new understanding of their needs, and her role in providing for them. Working closely with her teaching assistant, she began to uncover evidence from within her practice and context that at first shocked her, but later prompted her to reflect further and read widely. Her realisation that her pedagogy and her strategies in relation to providing appropriate support in the children's play were in need of some revision, prompted her into developing a completely different and new approach to her teaching.

> The biggest impact of the research has been on my professional development. My whole understanding of children's play, and the teacher's role in this has gained considerable insight . . . the weaknesses of the play opportunities that I was offering the children were exposed through this process of critical self-reflection (Carr and Kemmis, 1986; McNiff and Whitehead, 2002). The evidence from the action research cycle showed that taking a directive stance in play was of little benefit in comparison to active participation. The implications for my teaching would mean that I would have to change my whole approach when intervening in children's play.

Reflection 3

Miriam's project was undertaken in 2002, when support for science and technology teaching was still a key focus for staff development in primary schools. Despite fairly intense support for many schools in the preceding years, there was still some concern that teachers were not comfortable teaching these subjects and lacked the confidence to deal with certain aspects of subject knowledge. For many primary school science coordinators, improving the effectiveness of science and technology teaching and learning, both in terms of subject knowledge and an appropriate pedagogy, was a key priority.

Miriam had decided to undertake a review of the curriculum, and rewrite schemes of work in a shared way in the hope that she could use this as a vehicle to develop teachers' subject knowledge, pedagogy and, most importantly, their confidence.

> Initially I set out to improve the practice of science and technology teaching in our school. Early indications suggest that the outcomes are good. Teachers are more enthusiastic about teaching science and technology and this is evident by the discussions and debates I hear among staff. I feel I have developed a group of teachers who share ideas and share worries about teaching science and technology.

Reflection 4

Nicola's project derived from her work with some disaffected year 10 pupils who had a history of underachievement. In many cases they also had a poor record of homework completion and attendance. In her role as a member of the school leadership team (Manager for Teaching and Learning) her research focus centred around how she could lead the staff in finding out why these pupils were underachieving and, as a result of this, put in place measures to address the issue. Her first action step on the basis of an initial reconnaissance was to draw up a Pupil Learning Support Plan which staff helped implement and monitor. A core group of staff worked with her on this, setting targets for each of the pupils, based on their understanding of why pupils were underachieving. Early reflections on the implementation of this action step indicated to her that it did not seem to be working well. She asked teachers to assess the extent to which the pupils were meeting the targets, and discovered that there was little, if any, change in pupil behaviour, attendance or engagement with lessons and homework. More worrying for her, the teachers had adopted a stance of referring to them as 'Nicola's Group', describing them as 'unhelpable'. Having gained the opinions of the teachers, she decided to canvass the opinion of the pupils in order to see how well they felt they had met their targets. Comparing the two sets of opinions (the pupils' and the teachers') revealed very different stories, and from these different stories, she was prompted to talk in more depth to the pupils to try to better understand their views. It was at this stage that she really began to gain insight into the reasons for pupils' non-participation and realised that she needed to find ways in which to improve communication between staff and pupils in order to make any significant changes in pupil support strategies. She was also surprised to note just how significant classroom practice and culture are, and how even when seemingly small scale changes are made, their impact on pupils is considerable. This finding that she had not been looking for is the one which she considers important enough to share with colleagues.

Reflecting on her project she writes:

> I have learned that as teachers we make assumptions about what is best for the pupils we teach. These assumptions are based on what we believe the pupils need, and not what the pupils tell us they need. In my experience teachers very rarely talk to pupils about their needs. We assume that we know what the pupils need to do to achieve...we assume that if they do not achieve it is their fault....

She further notes that she would like to share her findings with all staff, to show them how 'their practice is effecting change no matter how small or difficult to observe in their daily teaching'.

Reflection 5

Carole's project had been undertaken in a special school, where she had been asked to lead the development of improved parental links with the school. There had been some unease in the school, with concerns around the extent, or lack, of parental involvement, the nature of that involvement, and the type of relationship that parents might, or indeed should, have with staff in the school. Her primary focus was to develop an approach to encourage more parental involvement, but also to improve the quality of it. She worked with groups of parents and staff, exploring the processes for parental involvement currently in place, discussing ways in which they worked, and ways in which they did not. Her reflections reveal not only her changed perspective in parental involvement, but also the impact her work had on her colleagues in school.

The question that faced my colleagues and I was, what could we do to try to change the nature of the relationship to one where parents felt empowered. This indicated that teachers would have to reflect on a personal level on the type of parent involvement they would be comfortable with. By changing the structures and procedures in place we discovered that parents did want to become involved in the life of the department as long as we provided a forum that enabled them to share their expertise. . . . as well as exploring, examining and questioning my beliefs and practice I had tried to encourage my colleagues to do the same. . . . by adopting an action research approach to the home–school partnership project we have strengthened the relationships between teaching staff also. Valuable time has now been given to staff to plan the way forward.

Commentary

These five reflective accounts illustrate a number of points. First they identify the relevance of action research to a range of issues and contexts:

- issues of teacher-pupil relationships
- the discovery and development of appropriate subject knowledge and pedagogy
- collaborative approaches to curriculum planning
- the role of pupil voice in planning to address underachievement
- the development of meaningful partnerships with parents.

It is not hard to extrapolate from this list the potential of action research in almost any situation in which a practitioner may find themselves. A desire to understand and improve that practice and situation is the most important prerequisite.

Secondly, the reflections presented also illustrate the way in which action research transcends a simple evaluation agenda, and explore some of the biggest moral and ethical issues in human relationships. Issues of power, democracy, respect, collaboration, voice and right action (all part of the accounts discussed) are but some of them. In your own work, you will have faced dilemmas in relation to some of these issues, you will have had to make judgement calls, knowing that there is no single right answer but that the answer you arrive at must be defensible. Thus you will have explored your own practice in a deeply meaningful and meaning-making way. In exploring issues identified by your own professional and personal needs, in the highly contextualised setting of your own practice you have explored the particularities of that practice, and thus its potential for improving. In subjecting this exploration to wider scholarship and research, you have also uncovered ways in which the particular speaks to the general, informing, relating, challenging and explaining. These are the things that make action research distinctive, and also make it important to share.

Lived experience, living theory

Many texts on action research take a 'lived experience' or 'living theory' approach, as we have already seen. A criticism of action research, which, I would argue, is always to some degree a lived experience or living theory approach, is that it is always concerned with the particular. Its perceived lack of generalisability is considered a weakness in many quarters, though as discussed in Chapter 6, Mejía (2010) challenges this, suggesting that generalisation is a continuing process in action research as we seek to produce something that can be shared, related and interrogated.

Reflection

Reflect on a time when you read a very personal or personalised account of someone's classroom or other practice. It may, for example, have been a case study produced as an illustrative example of some resource in practice. Why did you read it? What, if anything, did you gain from reading it? Do you usually read such case studies?

For most of us, reading accounts of other practice and other experiences resonates with our own experiences. We find ourselves agreeing or disagreeing with what we read. We make sense of what we read and, in doing so, start making sense of our own experiences also. This is even more the case when the accounts that we read contain issues that are universally important to us as human beings. While the context and substantive matter may have some relation to our own practical concerns, it is the bigger concepts within them that are particularly relevant and relatable to our own situation. Regardless of whether the context is in a pre-school setting where children are learning the protocols of socialisation, or the class of 16-year-old mathematics students or in the senior management team meeting in a college, issues of respect, right action and so forth are present, and of key importance. It could be argued that attention to values such as these will actually enable the development of appropriate actions.

It is precisely because of this value-base of action research, because of its desire to improve, that the reports produced, although having their genesis in the highly contextualised, have universal relatability. Their catalytic action in challenging us to interrogate our own practice similarly makes it vital that we share them. There is also, of course, a need to give voice to people and stories to validate their significance. Cook (2009) cites Seamus Heaney (1999): 'what is articulated strengthens itself and what is not articulated tends towards non-being' and, in doing so, reminds us that without making things known in this way, discussion and debate around them is not possible.

A further point illustrated by these reflections is the way in which action research brings unexpected findings and, with them, unexpected value to the whole process. Miriam, Nicola and Carole all find unanticipated outcomes. Miriam, in attempting to produce a new scheme of work, finds that she has precipitated the development of a more collaborative approach to work among her colleagues. Nicola realises just how significant an impact teachers' practices can have on pupils, while Carole finds that in trying to improve relationships with parents, staff relationships have improved also.

It is for all these reasons that teachers and other practitioners owe it to themselves, and their colleagues, to share and promote action research. To do so is not always easy though, and if the promotion and sharing of action research is to be encouraged, then creative ways of doing so need to be found.

How we should share action research accounts

In Chapter 2, I suggested that the findings from an action research project 'may be disseminated orally, in written reports or indeed in other ways'. It is now time to discuss some of those other ways. Throughout this book, the presumption has been that most readers are likely to be engaged in academic study, and completing written reports as part of the assessment cycle. While it is common practice for students on such courses to submit fairly standard written reports, it is by no means universal. Other options exist, and in some cases students may be guided towards these. However the report is produced, it will be shared to some degree through the assessment processes. While this sharing may be on a relatively small scale, it is still important to recognise it as such. Tutors can often benefit professionally and academically from reading such reports and, in turn, share their learning with colleagues. The ways in which our accounts may influence others can seem small, or even non-existent, and in a culture where 'impact' is measured for each and every initiative, often as soon as the initiative has been completed, the concept of slowly filtering influence can be overlooked. Saunders (2011) finds the term 'impact' harsh and challenging, more congruent with 'road crashes and war mongering', and inappropriate in the discourse of human behaviour. Suggesting that 'influence' is a more appropriate term, she discusses its etymology as coming from the the Latin *influere*, to flow into (Saunders, 2011: 16). While she acknowledges that there is a potential for such discussion to be seen as word play, she clearly outlines the power of words and metaphors in shaping our thoughts and actions, suggesting that:

> the idea of 'impact' in research is in danger of preventing us from exploring and understanding the human – that is, the social and psychological and political and economic – processes that we must understand in order to participate in, and intervene on, them. Metaphors have a bearing on how researchers approach the task of making their epistemic efforts known and felt in the world. (Saunders, 2011: 117)

Drawing on this concept of 'influence' as flow, and in the knowledge that such flow is part and parcel of academic life as tutors interact with, teach and learn from their students, I first explore the assessment of action research reports as a form of sharing and dissemination.

Rather than focus on the academic essay, which in some respects is relatively unproblematic for assessment purposes, I want instead to consider some of the other ways in which action research may be reported and assessed. In many cases, these assessment tasks are shared with a relatively small audience and, in the case of some formats, may only be shared with the examining tutor. It *is* a form of sharing though, and its influence may be unpredictable in both size and significance.

Sharing action research through assessment processes

In many ways, the choice of dissemination mode is very much dependent on the context. The focus in Chapter 7 on producing a written account is based on a need to do so for assessment requirements. Alternative modes of reporting may also be allowed for assessment, so we will first explore these.

When action research is assessed in academic programmes, the assessment criteria will indicate that it is the articulation of the process itself, the reflections and scholarly deliberations on it, and the ways in which it has informed professional learning that are the key criteria. Whether the project achieved its intended outcome is not, in this context, particularly important. What is important is the level and quality of engagement with the process. For this reason, alternatives to the 'academic essay' may be used in assessment (or indeed other) contexts. Among these alternatives are:

- oral presentation supported by slides and notes
- poster presentation supported by notes
- the production of a paper suitable for an academic or professional journal
- a conference presentation
- patchwork text.

These will usually, though not always, be accompanied by a written reflection. I briefly consider each in turn.

Presentation

This mode of assessment allows students to more easily present images or other media artefacts as part of a portfolio of evidence in their project. The use of presentation software such as PowerPoint™ or Prezi™ can provide an opportunity to show many aspects of their project in more creative ways. Jack Whitehead, in many of his recent writings (available at actionresearch.net) and in his YouTube™ channel (where, at last count, he had over 400 clips available) advocates the use of video to illustrate human values in living theory.

If oral presentation or video clip is an option for you, then it would be worthwhile looking at Jack's clips. For many people, the production of slide presentations, or video clips, generates a very real potential for a 'style over substance' approach. As in any communication mode, the purpose and audience must guide the 'voice'. Jack's videos are an excellent example of how the technology is used with a 'no frills' approach to simply capture the essence of what is happening and being illustrated. In this way, the substance of his message is given priority of place, while the technology is simply a mode of transmission. The fact that the video can convey more than the actual text of the transaction is important in Jack's work, and his use of video is chosen as a fit-for-purpose mode in many cases.

Thus, in preparing media of any sort, from slides to video, audio or still images, it is important to remember that they are the carriers of the message, and not the message itself. While it is of course appropriate to ensure that their 'presentation' is executed well and engagingly, the main thing to remember is the message itself. With some careful thought, and the need to meet the time limits normally imposed, the opportunity to present orally may help in distilling key points and analyses from the project. Further, it is often the case that for academic assessment purposes, such presentations may require an accompanying piece of reflective writing, which can support the development of a more critically reflective and analytic engagement with the project, and thus enable the student to meet the academic assessment criteria.

Poster presentation

Like oral presentations, posters can be a means of presenting material that does not easily lend itself to the 'academic essay'. The opportunity to creatively and appropriately put together a report that benefits from images, mind maps and other diagrammatics can be of enormous benefit to the researcher struggling to describe a multilayered, multifaceted research project. Like oral presentations also, they almost force a level of analysis in that they limit space. Each word, diagram or image must be chosen carefully in order to optimise the space available. Many poster presentation events also provide a chance for the researcher to interact with 'the viewers', and in that way discuss, debate and field questions on the project. This in itself becomes a learning process for the presenter, as they defend, or possibly change, their analyses and interpretations.

Journal paper

Increasingly, students are offered opportunities to publish their work, or, more usually, produce it in publishable format, usually by writing it in the 'house style' of a particular journal or forum. As with other less traditional academic essay approaches, a short supporting paper may be required in relation to academic assessment criteria. It well may be the case, though, that the paper alone can satisfy assessment criteria. In any case, whether the article is actually submitted for publication or not, is not usually part of the assessment requirements (on a purely pragmatic level, the submission-to-publication timescale would be prohibitive) – merely that it could be assessed as suitable for publication.

Conference paper/presentation

When offered as an assessment option, the conference in question will usually be specially organised for the programme. It may be conducted along the lines of an external conference in that students will have to submit an abstract in advance, perhaps receiving some feedback on it following a review process. They will then present their completed work at the conference to a group of their colleagues and tutors. Again, the limits placed in terms of presentation time require a careful and focused preparation, carefully selecting the most important information.

Patchwork text

This approach was developed by Richard Winter, and explored in his 2003 paper 'Contextualizing the patchwork text: addressing problems of coursework assessment in higher education'. Arguing that in many cases, traditional academic essays fail to deliver in relation to the need for deep reflective learning, he proposes a patchwork approach which 'consists of a variety of small sections, each of which is complete in itself, and that the overall unity of these component sections, although planned in advance, is finalized retrospectively, when they are "stitched together"' (Winter, 2003: 112).

While the decision to present a report in patchwork format is not one which can be made retrospectively, in that it is best supported by a congruent teaching and supervision approach, it is an approach that lends itself to a high degree of personalisation, and resonates with Lave's concept of doing and knowing as 'inventive . . . They are open-ended processes of improvisation with the social, material and experiential resources at hand' (Lave, 1993: 13). If you have arrived at a final extended study or dissertation module in your postgraduate programme, and feel that this might be a suitable approach, then it is important that you confirm with your tutor or supervisor that it will be acceptable within the assessment framework. It is also important to have the support of a sympathetic tutor or supervisor in the development of the study.

Reflection

Consider an action research project you are either currently or were recently involved in. If you had total freedom to construct a report of the project, what mode of presentation might you use, and why? Consider why your chosen mode is better than the others, but consider also whether it has any weaknesses.

Other ways to share action research

Arguably, any report of action research that is completed is a form of sharing and dissemination. However, the audience is fairly limited, unless larger groups are invited to presentations and conferences, or written reports are shared through journals, websites or other means. For this reason, action researchers often find other means to share and promote their work. In the previous section we discussed the use of journal publication and conference presentation in relation to assessment requirements. We will now consider some of the other ways in which action researchers can share and disseminate their work.

Collaboration in schools and settings

For many practitioners, this will be the key way in which they share their work. At the lowest level of sharing, colleagues and pupils will probably have been involved in the generation of data. Interviews, questionnaires, observations and so forth will all have been negotiated in relation to the project, and participants will be aware that it is happening. Informal professional conversations will allow the researcher to raise awareness of the project. In some cases, however, colleagues and/or pupils become more deeply involved with the project, more proactively generating data for it and, in doing so, become more like co-researchers than research participants. When this type of sharing happens, those co-researchers become inducted into the processes of action research themselves. In this way, they begin to learn the potential and potency of action research.

Action researchers often have an opportunity, or increasingly (when schools are providing financial and other support for teachers undertaking such programmes) an obligation, to make a presentation to a group of staff, or governors. This generates conversations around the research, the sharing of any recommendations for any further actions or research, and gives voice and recognition to the researcher, thus validating their work.

External conferences and networks

A number of external networking opportunities exists where action researchers can share and discuss their work. The Collaborative Action Research Network (CARN), 'aims to encourage and support action research projects (personal, local, national and international), accessible accounts of action research projects, and contributions to the theory and methodology of action research.' (http://www.esri.mmu. ac.uk/carnnew/). Its annual conference provides support for action researchers, a forum for the sharing and discussion of emerging ideas or dilemmas in the research. Membership of the network provides an opportunity to keep such conversations going.

Other professional networks and organisations exist, with many having particular support for students in the form of a special student/novice researcher conference. The British Educational Research Association (BERA) is one such, with its Early Career Researcher Conference which aims to:

- provide early career researchers with the opportunity to present papers to an audience of fellow early career researchers;
- offer sessions on research processes led by experienced researchers, e.g. on interviewing, data analysis, writing skills, presentation techniques;
- help early career researchers develop a network of contacts. (http://bera conference.co.uk/)

All such conferences welcome 'work in progress' so there is no need for a fully completed piece of work in order to present. Many (like BERA) also offer dedicated research support for early stage researchers. In my experience, the conference is at its most useful when the presentation is a work in progress. Not only does it provide a forum for sharing, but it also provides an opportunity for questioning and feedback on your developing work so that the whole experience feeds back into the project, assisting understanding and analysis. A supportive conference experience such as this engenders a sense of belonging to a community of critical friends, which can support the development of further research projects. Such networks of critical friends can be further developed through the use of associated (or other) online discussion sites and forums, where the reach is potentially global.

Publication

Many professional journals are very happy to publish accounts of practitioner action research, and of the academic journals, titles such as *Reflective Practice* and *Educational Action Research* (both published by Taylor and Francis), and *Action Research* (published by Sage) may well consider such pieces. Likewise, the *Educational Journal of Living Theories* (*EJOLTS*), published online at http://ejolts.net welcomes accounts of 'personal journeys and collaborative pathways that explain educational influences in learning in terms of values, skills and understandings that the researcher believes carries hope for the future of humanity and their own'.

A range of other publication opportunities occurs through the journals, magazines and websites of professional associations that teachers may belong to. These will generally have less rigorous reviewing procedures than the more academic journals, but with potentially a much wider readership, are an excellent means by which to share action research accounts. Some schools or school clusters may also produce their own magazines, which again can disseminate the work to a broader community.

Summary

It can be seen that sharing action research accounts is an important part of the process itself. Echoing the democratic and democratising nature of the process, it enhances the professional learning and development of those who share and those who are shared with. The means by which this sharing can be done are wide-ranging, and can be chosen to suit the needs of the researcher and the needs of the professional community in which the research took place, and do not need to be highly formalised or challenging for the new action researcher. While teachers and other education practitioners may find that their main requirement to share is through assessment or other relatively formal techniques, they should be encouraged to disseminate their work through a range of other, often informal, mechanisms.

Saunders (2001), in describing an e-learning project she was involved in along with Bridget Somekh, discusses the wide range of formal, semi-formal and often relatively informal ways in which the work was disseminated, explaining how it took place

> through seminars, draft working papers, face-to-face conversations and online discussions rather than through the performative production of a text, the 'final report'. What happened can be construed as a continual re-invention, rather than a closing-down, of the research, and the work subsequently came to have an unforeseen relevance in critically examining the then government's agenda for 'personalised learning'. (Saunders, 2011: 117)

In many ways, the more creative and tentative mechanisms both echo and enhance action research's dynamic nature, bringing further opportunities for reflection and unanticipated learning.

Further reading

Given the nature of this chapter, and the exhortation to share action research accounts in a variety of ways it is appropriate to suggest some websites as sources of further reading.

Richard Winter's site, http://www.richardwinter.net, hosts an archive of his work, much of which will be of interest to school-based action researchers.

Jack Whitehouse's site, actionresearch.net and his youtube™ channel http://www.youtube.com/user/JackWhitehead, both host a vast archive of his work and, in particular, the video footage presents an alternative articulation and presentation of action research.

The following may also be of help throughout the action research process. All have resources and readings which will be of use, and also links to other sites:

Teacher Action Research, http://gse.gmu.edu/research/tr/

Action Research Websites, http://www2.alliance.brown.edu/dnd/ar_websites.shtml

Centre for Collaborative Action Research, http://cadres.pepperdine.edu/ccar/resources.html

Additional online resources can be found at: www.sagepub.co.uk/beraseries.sp

REFERENCES

Adams, T. (2008) 'A review of narrative ethics', *Qualitative Inquiry*, 14(2): 175–94.

Altrichter, H. and Posch, P. (1992) *Teachers Investigate their Work: An Introduction to the Methods of Action Research*, English trans. L. P. Posch. Abingdon: Routledge.

Altrichter, H., Feldman, A., Posch, P. and Somekh, B. (2008) *Teachers Investigate Their Work: An Introduction to Action Research across the Professions*. Abingdon: Routledge.

Angelides, P. (2001) 'The development of an efficient technique for collecting and analyzing qualitative data: the analysis of critical incidents', *Qualitative Studies in Education*, 14(3): 429–42.

Attard, K. (2012) 'The role of narrative writing in improving professional practice', *Educational Action Research*, 20(1): 161–75.

Austen, J. (1994) *Emma*. London: Penguin.

Bassey, M. (2001) 'A solution to the problem of generalisation in educational research: fuzzy prediction', *Oxford Review of Education*, 27(1): 5–22.

Baumfield, V., Hall, E. and Wall, K. (2008) *Action Research in the Classroom*. London: Sage.

Benjamin, M. (1991) *Science and Sensibility, Gender and Scientific Enquiry (1780–1945)*. Oxford: Blackwell.

BERA (2011) *Ethical Guidelines for Educational Research*. Available at: http://www.bera.ac.uk/publications/ethical-guidelines (accessed February 2012).

Bernstein, R.J. (1983). *Beyond Objectivism and Relativism: Science, Hermeneutics and Praxis*. Oxford: Basil Blackwell.

Bold, C. (2012) *Using Narrative in Research*. London: Sage.

Bolton, G. (2005) *Reflective Practice: Writing and Professional Development*. London: Sage.

Bridges, D. (2003) 'A philosopher in the classroom', *Educational Action Research*, 11(2): 181–96.

Bridges, D. (2007) 'Professionalism, authenticity and action research', *Educational Action Research*, 9(3): 451–64.

Briggs, J. (1992) *Fractals: The Patterns of Chaos*. London: Thames & Hudson.

Broad, W. and Wade, N. (1985) *Betrayers of the Truth: Fraud and Deceit in Science*. Oxford: Oxford University Press.

Brookfield, S. (1995) *Becoming a Critically Reflective Teacher*. San Francisco: Jossey-Bass.

Burton, D. and Bartlett, S. (2009) *Key Issues for Education Researchers*. London: Sage.

Cain, T. (2011) 'Teachers' classroom-based action research', *International Journal of Research & Method in Education*, 34(1): 3–16.

Campbell, A. and Groundwater-Smith, S. (eds) (2010) *Connecting Inquiry and Professional Learning in Education: International Perspectives and Practical Solutions*. Oxford: Routledge.

Carr, W. (1980) 'The gap between theory and practice', *The Journal of Further and Higher Education*, 4(1).

Carr, W. (1987) 'What is an Educational Practice?', paper presented at the Annual Conference of the Philosophy of Education Society of Great Britain, London, April.

Carr, W. (2005) 'The role of theory in the professional development of an educational theorist', *Pedagogy, Culture and Society*, 13(3).

Carr, W. (2005a) 'Philosophy, methodology and action research', paper presented at the Practitioner Research/Collaborative Action Research Conference, Utrecht, November.

Carr, W. (2006) 'Philosophy, methodology and action research', *Journal of Philosophy of Education*, 40(4): 421–35.

Carr, W. (2007) 'Educational research as a practical science', *International Journal of Research & Method in Education*, 30(3): 271–86.

Carr, W. and Kemmis, S. (1986) *Becoming Critical: Education, Knowledge and Action Research*. London: Falmer Press.

Chambers, D. (1983) 'Stereotypical images of the scientist: the Draw-a-Scientist test', *Science Education*, (67): 255–65.

Clough, P. (2002) *Narratives and Fictions in Educational Research*. Buckingham and Philadelphia, PA: Open University Press.

Cook, T. (1998) 'The importance of mess in action research', *Educational Action Research*, 6(1): 93–109.

Cook, T. (2009) 'The purpose of mess in action research: building rigour though a messy turn', *Educational Action Research*, 17(2): 277–91.

Corey, S. (1953) *Action Research to Improve School Practices*. New York: Teachers College Press.

Cornett, J.W. (1995) 'The importance of systematic reflection: implications of a naturalistic model of research', *Anthropology and Education Quarterly*, 26: 123–9.

Crotty, M. (1998) *The Foundations of Social Research*. London: Sage.

Dadds, M. (1995) *Passionate Inquiry and School Development: A Story about Teacher Action Research*. London: Falmer Press.

Dadds, M. and Hart, S. (2001) *Doing Practitioner Research Differently*. London: RoutledgeFalmer.

Dana, N.F. (2009) *Leading with Passion and Knowledge: The Principal as Action Researcher*. Thousand Oaks, CA: Corwin Press.

Davies, J. (2007) 'Rethinking the architecture: an action researcher's resolution to writing and presenting their thesis', *Action Research*, 5(2): 181–98.

Day, C. (1993) 'Reflection: a necessary but not sufficient condition for professional development', *British Educational Research Journal*, 19(1): 83–94.

Department for Education (DfE) (2010) *The Importance of Teaching: Schools White Paper*. CM 7980. London: The Stationery Office.

Dick, B. (2000) 'A beginner's guide to action research'. Available at: http://www.scu.edu.au/schools/gcm/ar/arp/guide.html (accessed 29 September 2012).

Edgeworth, M. and Edgeworth, R.L. (1798) *Practical Education*. London.

Elliott, J. (1978) 'What is action research in schools?', *The Journal of Curriculum Studies*, 10(4): 355–7.

Elliott, J. (1981) *A Framework for Self Evaluation in Schools*. Cambridge: Cambridge University Press.

Elliott, J. (1991) *Action Research for Educational Change*. Milton Keynes: Open University Press.

Elliott, J. (1994) 'Developing community-focused environmental education through action research', in B. Somekh and M. Pettigrew (eds), *Evaluating Innovation in Environmental Education*. Paris: OECD. pp. 31–60.

Elliott, J. (1996) 'Bringing action research home', paper presented at EERA Conference, New York.

Elliott, J. (1997) *The Curriculum Experiment, Meeting the Challenge of Social Change*. Buckingham: Open University Press.

Elliott, J. (2000) 'Doing action research, doing philosophy', *Prospero*, 6: 82–100.

Elliott, J. (2007) 'Assessing the quality of action research', *Research Papers in Education*, 22(2): 229–46.

Evans, M. (1997) 'Shifting the leadership focus from control to empowerment: a case study', *School Leadership and Management*, 17(2): 273–83.

Feldman, A. (1994) 'Ertzberger's Dilemma: Validity in action research and science teachers need to know', *Science Education*, 78(1): 83–101.

Feldman, A. (2007) 'Validity and quality in action research', *Educational Action Research*, 15(1): 21–32.

Flanders, N.A. (1970) *Analysing Teaching Behaviour*. Reading, MA: Addison-Wesley.

Gadamer, H.G. (1975) *Truth and Method*. London: Sheed & Ward.

Geertz, C. (1973) *The Interpretation of Cultures*. New York: Basic.

Ghaye, A. and Ghaye, K. (1998) *Teaching and Learning through Critical Reflective Practice*. London: David Fulton.

Green, K. (1999) 'Defining the field of literature in action research: a personal approach', *Educational Action Research*, 7(1): 105–24.

Griffiths, M. and Tann, S. (1991) 'Ripples in the reflection', in P. Lomax (ed.), *BERA Dialogues*, no. 5: 82–101.

Groundwater-Smith, S. and Mockler, N. (2006) 'Research that counts: practitioner research and the academy', in *Counterpoints on the Quality and Impact of Educational Research, Special Edition of Review of Australian Research in Education*, 6: 105–17.

Hammersley, M. (2006) 'Philosophy, who needs it? The case of social science research on education', *Journal of Philosophy of Education*, 40(2): 273–86.

Heikkinen, H., Huttunen, R. and Syrjälä, L. (2007) 'Action research as narrative: five principles for validation in 2'. *Educational Action Research*, 15(1): 5–19.

Hutchinson, B. and Whitehouse, P. (1999) 'The impact of action research and education reform in Northern Ireland: education in democracy', *British Educational Research Journal*, 25(2): 141–55.

Johnson, A.P. (2008) *A Short Guide to Action Research*. Boston, MA: Allyn & Bacon.

Johnson, A.P. (2009) *A Short Guide to Action Research*. 3rd edn. Boston, MA: Allyn & Bacon.

Kemmis, S. (2005) 'Knowing practice', *Pedagogy, Culture and Society*, 13(3): 391.

Kemmis, S. (2007) 'Action research', in M. Hammersley (ed.), *Educational Research and Evidence-Based Practice*. Milton Keynes: Open University Press. pp. 167–80.

Kemmis, S. and McTaggart, R. (1981) *The Action Research Planner*. Victoria: Deakin University Press.

Kuhn, T.S. (1970) *The Structure of Scientific Revolutions*. London: University of Chicago Press.

Lave, J. (1993) 'The practice of learning', in S. Chaiklin and J. Lave (eds), *Understanding Practice: Perspectives on Activity and Context*. Cambridge: Cambridge University Press.

MacIntyre, A.C. (1981) *After Virtue: A Study in Moral Philosophy*. London: Duckworth.

Malpas, J., Ulrich, A. and Kertscher, J. (eds) (2002) *Gadamer's Century: Essays in Honour of Hans-Georg Gadamer*. Cambridge, MA: MIT Press.

Mason, C., Butler Kahle, J. and Gardner, A. (1991) 'Draw-a-Scientist test: future implications', *School Science and Mathematics*, (91): 193–8.

Mason, J. (2002) *Researching Your Own Practice: The Discipline of Noticing*. London: RoutledgeFalmer.

McAteer, M. (2012) 'Theory generative approaches in practitioner research', in J. Adams, M. Cochrane and L. Dunne (eds), *Applying Theory to Educational Research*. Oxford: Blackwell.

McAteer, M. and Dewhurst, J. (2010) '"Just thinking about stuff": reflective learning: Jane's story', *Reflective Practice: International and Multidisciplinary Perspectives*, 11(1): 33–43.

McAteer, M. and Wilkinson, M. (2009) 'Evaluating the efficacy of training staff in adult child interaction in a school for children with ASD', *Journal of Good Autism Practice*, 10(2): 57–63.

McAteer, M., Hallett, F., Murtagh, L. and Turnbull, G. (2010) *Achieving your Masters in Teaching and Learning*. Exeter: Learning Matters.

McKernan, J. (1997) *Curriculum Action Research: A Handbook of Methods and Resources for the Reflective Practitioner*. London: Kogan Page.

McMahon, T. and Jefford, E. (2009) 'Assessing action-research projects within formal academic programmes: using Elliott's context-related criteria to resolve the rigour versus flexibility dilemma', *Educational Action Research*, 17(3): 359–71.

McNiff, J. (2002) *Action Research for Professional Development*. 3rd edn. Available at: http://jeanmcniff.com/ar-booklet.asp (accessed 29 September 2012).

McNiff, J., with Whitehead, J. (2002) *Action Research: Principles and Practice*. 2nd edn. London: Routledge.

McTaggart, R. (1996) 'Issues for participatory action researchers', in O. Zuber-Skerritt (ed.), *New Directions in Action Research*. London: Falmer. pp. 242–55.

Mejía, A. (2010) 'The general in the particular', *Journal of Philosophy of Education*, 44(1): 93–107.

Mellor, N. (2001) 'Messy method: the unfolding story', *Educational Action Research*, 9(3): 465–84.

Mertler, C. (2009) *Action Research: Teachers as Researchers in the Classroom*. Thousand Oaks, CA: Sage.

Miles, M.B. and Huberman, A.M. (1994) *Qualitative Data Analysis*. 2nd edn. Newbury Park, CA: Sage. pp. 10–12.

Milton, R. (1994) *Forbidden Science, Suppressed Research that Could Change our Lives*. London: Fourth Estate.

Moon, J. (2006) *A Handbook of Reflective and Experiential Learning: Theory and Practice*. London: RoutledgeFalmer.

'National Scholarship Scheme in 2011'. www.tda.gov.uk/pdscholarship (site now down).

Oancea, O. and Furlong, J. (2007) 'Expressions of excellence and the assessment of applied and practice-based research', *Research Papers in Education*, 22(2): 119–37.

Popper, K. (1959) *The Logic of Scientific Discovery*. London: Hutchinson.

Popper, K. (1968) *The Logic of Scientific Discovery*. 2nd edn. London: Hutchinson .

Popper, K. (1972) *Objective Knowledge: An Evolutionary Approach*. Oxford: Clarendon Press.

Poulson, L. and Wallace, M. (2004) *Learning to Read Critically in Teaching and Learning*. London: Sage.

Pring, R. (2000) *Philosophy of Educational Research*. London: Continuum.

Punch, K.F. (1998) *Introduction to Social Research: Quantitative and Qualitative Approaches*. London: Sage.

Reason, P. and Bradbury, H. (2006) *Handbook of Action Research: The Concise Paperback Edition*. London: Sage.

Reason, P. and Torbert, W. R. (2001) 'The action turn: toward a transformational social science', *Concepts and Transformation*, 6(1): 1–37.

Riding, P., Fowell, S. and Levy, P. (1995) 'An action research approach to curriculum development', *Information Research*, 1(1).

Robson, C.R. (2002) *Real World Research*. 2nd edn. Oxford: Blackwell.

Rolfe, G. (2001) *Knowledge and Practice*. London: Distance Learning Centre.

Saunders, L. (2004) 'Evidence-led professional creativity: a perspective from the General Teaching Council for England', *Educational Action Research*, 12(1): 163–8.

Saunders, L. (2007) 'An alternative way of responding to powerful ideas: notes to accompany the poem entitled "Five Principles of Quality in Narratives of Action Research"', *Educational Action Research*, 15(1): 33–40.

Saunders, L. (2011) 'Road crashes and war-mongering: why the notion of "impact" in research is wrong', *Research Intelligence*, Spring (114): 16–17.

Schön, D.A. (1983) *The Reflective Practitioner, How Professionals Think in Action*. London: Temple Smith.

Sheldrake, R. (1994) *Seven Experiments That Could Change the World*. London: Fourth Estate.

Smith, P. (1963) *Philosophy of Education*. New York: Harper & Row.

Smyth, J. (1991) *Teachers as Collaborative Learners*. Milton Keynes: Open University Press.

Stark, R. (1998) 'Practitioner research: the purposes of reviewing the literature within an enquiry'. Available at: http://cartl.pbworks.com/f/Reviewing+the+literature.pdf.pdf (accessed March 2012).

Stenhouse, L. (1975) *An Introduction to Curriculum Research and Development*. London: Heinemann.

Strauss, A. and Corbin, J. (1990) Basics of Qualitative Research: Grounded Theory Procedures and Techniques. London: Sage.

Swartz, M.R. (1992) 'Reexamination of the key cold fusion experiment by the MIT Plasma Fusion Laboratory', *Fusion Facts* (newsletter of the Fusion Information Center, University of Utah), 4(2): 27–34.

Thomas, G. (2009) *How to do Your Research Project: A Guide for Students in Education and Applied Social Sciences*. London: Sage.

Tripp, D. (1993) *Critical Incidents In Teaching: Developing Professional Judgement*. London: Routledge.

Vandenbroucke, J. (2006) 'Observational research, randomised trials, and two views of medical science', *PLOS Medicine*. Available at: http://www.plosmedicine.org/article/info%3Adoi%2F10.1371%2Fjournal.pmed.0050067 (accessed January 2012).

Whitehead, J. (1993) *The Growth of Educational Knowledge*. Bournemouth: Hyde Publications.

Winter, R. (1987) *Action Research and the Nature of Social Inquiry: Professional Innovation and Educational Work*. Aldershot: Avebury.

Winter, R. (2003) 'The patchwork text: a radical re-assessment of coursework assignments', *Innovations in Education and Teaching International*, special issue, 40(2): 112–22.

Winter, R., with Griffiths, M. and Green, K. (2000) 'The "academic" qualities of practice': what are the criteria for a practice-based PhD?', *Studies in Higher Education*, 25(1): 25–37.

Wood, L. (2010) 'The transformative potential of living theory educational research', *Educational Journal of Living Theories*, 3(1): 115–18.

Woods, P. (1993) 'Critical incidents in education', *British Journal of Sociology of Education*, 14(4): 355–71.

Zeichner, K.M. (1993) 'Action research: personal renewal and social reconstruction', *Educational Action Research*, 1(2): 199–219.

Action research websites

http://www2.alliance.brown.edu/dnd/ar_websites.shtml

www.aral.com.au

British Educational Research Association (BERA), http://beraconference.co.uk/

Centre for Collaborative Action Research at Pepperdine University, http://cadres.pepperdine.edu/ccar/about.html

Centre for Practitioner Research at National-Louis University, http://www.nl.edu/cfpr/resources/websites.cfm

Collaborative Action Research Network (CARN), http://www.esri.mmu.ac.uk/carnnew/

Council of European Social Science Data Archives, http://www.cessda.org

Dick, B. (2000) 'A beginner's guide to action research'. Available at: http://www.scu.edu.au/schools/gcm/ar/arp/guide.html

Educational Journal of Living Theories (EJOLTS), http://ejolts.net

http://guides.lib.purdue.edu/content.php?pid=219836&sid=1825694

McNiff, J. (2002) http://jeanmcniff.com/ar-booklet.asp

www.jeanmcniff.com

Teacher Action Research, http://gse.gmu.edu/research/tr/

Teaching and Learning Research Programme, http://www.tlrp.org

Whitehead, J., http://www.youtube.com/user/JackWhitehead

Whitehead, J., www.actionresearch.net

Winter, R., http://www.richardwinter.net

INDEX

Added to a page number 'f' denotes a figure and 't' denotes a table.